TO BE JESUS CRUCIFIED

CONCEPCIÓN CABRERA DE ARMIDA

TO BE JESUS CRUCIFIED

Retreat Directed by Archbishop Luis M. Martínez
1928

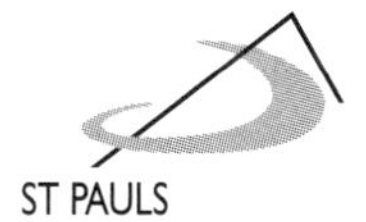

Original Spanish title: *Ser Jesús Crucificado,*
Ejercicios Espirituales 1928, Ediciones Cimiento, México
Presentation and Commentary
Clara Eugenia Labarthe, RCSCJ

Translated, edited and annotated for the English edition by
Sr. Elzbieta Sadowska, RCSCJ and Msgr. Arthur B. Calkins.

Cover: Fr. Eugenio Cárdenas Ramos, Missionary of the Holy Spirit

Library of Congress Cataloging-in-Publication Data

Conchita, 1862-1937.
[Ser Jesús Crucificado. English]
To be Jesus crucified: retreat directed by Archbishop Luis M. Martínez, 1928 / Concepción Cabrera de Armida.
pages cm
"Translated, edited, and annotated for the English edition by Sr. Elzbieta Sadowska, RCSCJ and Msgr. Arthur B. Calkins"—T.p. verso.
Includes bibliographical references.
ISBN 978-0-8189-1354-9
1. Spiritual life—Catholic Church. 2. Martinez, Luis M. (Luis Maria). 1881-1956—Sermons. 3. Spiritual retreats. 4. Jesus Christ. I. Martinez, Luis M. (Luis Maria), 1881-1956. II. Sadowska, Elzbieta. III. Calkins, Arthur Burton. IV. Title.
BX2350.3.C66313 2013
269'.6—dc23
2012046938

Nihil Obstat
Rafael Ledezma, M.Sp.S.
Jesús María, S.L.P., Mexico
August 7, 1996

Imprimatur
Melecio Picazo, M.Sp.S.
August, 1996

Produced and designed in the United States of America by the
Fathers and Brothers of the Society of St. Paul,
2187 Victory Boulevard, Staten Island, New York 10314-6603
as part of their communications apostolate.

ISBN 10: 0-8189-1354-1
ISBN 13: 978-0-8189-1354-9

Printing Information:

Current Printing - first digit 1 2 3 4 5 6 7 8 9 10

Year of Current Printing - first year shown

2013 2014 2015 2016 2017 2018 2019 2020 2021 2022

ACKNOWLEDGMENTS

Our heartfelt gratitude to
Msgr. Arthur B. Calkins for theological consultation,
to Fr. David Jones, Mr. James Wierzbicki,
and to all who have collaborated in the preparation of this book.

TABLE OF CONTENTS

PRESENTATION

While there are many themes that the discerning reader will discover in this "retreat notebook" of the Venerable Conchita and that the introduction mentions, I would like to call particular attention to two motifs that emerge in a striking way in this notebook as well as in many other writings of Conchita: that of the offering of Jesus to the Father and that of the offering of oneself in union with Him. These topics are absolutely fundamental to the Christian life and to Catholic worship. Indeed, ever since the publication of the Second Vatican Council's *Constitution on the Sacred Liturgy* there has been great emphasis on the active participation of the faithful in the Church's liturgy, especially the holy sacrifice of the Mass. Unfortunately, this has most often been understood in terms of external activities such as congregational singing and responding at Mass and the particular roles of lectors, cantors, choirs and servers.

The fundamental meaning of active participation, however, has to do with the priestly service of offering Jesus to the Father. This is the principal office of both the priest and the faithful at every Mass. True, there is an essential difference between the role of the ordained priest and that of the faithful in this highest act of Christian worship, but both priest and people are meant to be consciously involved in the offering of Jesus to the Father and the offering of themselves in union with Him for the salvation of the world. This is the very essence of Christian liturgy, but it seems to me that this is not sufficiently preached and taught. Nonetheless, even before the explicit magisterial teaching about this in the twentieth century by the Venerable Pius XII in his great Encyclical Letter on the Liturgy *Mediator Dei* of 20 November 1947 and in the Second Vatican Council's *Constitution on the Sacred Liturgy* of 4 December 1963, this teaching was being communicated to the Venerable Conchita and absorbed by her.

Not only is this concept of utmost importance in liturgy, but also in life. It provides the basis for the morning offering promoted by the Apostleship of Prayer. All of us can be involved in offering all of our prayers, works, joys and sufferings – everything but our sins – to the Father in union with Jesus for our salvation and that of the whole world. Conchita's great exemplar and tutor in this way of life was none other than the Mother of God who on Calvary offered Jesus to the Father and herself in union with Him. The grace of the Mystical Incarnation likened her to Mary very explicitly. May we also have the grace to live this life and so be transformed into Jesus crucified!

Msgr. Arthur B. Calkins

INTRODUCTION

Born in San Luis Potosí, Mexico, in a well-to-do and very pious Catholic family, the Venerable Concepción Cabrera de Armida, familiarly known as Conchita, (8 December 1862 - 3 March 1937), was a married woman, mother of nine children, foundress of the five Works of the Cross[1] and possibly the greatest mystic of the Mexican Church. Her parents, Don Octaviano Cabrera Lacavex and Clara Arias Rivera, were the owners of many *haciendas*, where Conchita passed her childhood and youth with her eleven brothers and sisters. In her *Account of Conscience*[2] Conchita wrote: "My parents were excellent Christians. In the *haciendas* [her family's country estates in Mexico] my father always prayed the rosary with the family and farm workers in the chapel." Her mother used to take all the children to visit the Blessed Sacrament. She taught them "doctrine, prayers and to do good." From her youth Conchita was greatly inclined to prayer, penance and, above all, to purity. Conchita's life was filled with extraordinary penances because she felt "great self-contempt and vehement hunger for suffering."

At the age of twenty-two, on November 8, 1884, she married Francisco Armida. Neither the nine years of courtship nor the seventeen years of marriage distracted her from God nor hindered her spiritual life. On the contrary, God Himself was present with more intensity in her life after her wedding, because she had been chosen as an instrument to show His power in "a soul who allows Him to fashion it." Her longing to belong to Jesus grew steadily. To her great surprise, precisely in the milieu of family life, "the Lord made Himself present with extraordinary and numerous graces."[3] Conchita lived her intense life of prayer, penance and charity on behalf of those in need and carried out her mission as a mystical writer in a silent and hidden way. Her husband died of typhoid fever on September 17, 1901. At the age of thirty-nine she became a widow with eight children (her second son, Carlos, died of typhoid fever in 1893).

Buoyed up by special graces, she managed to combine the activity of a foundress and mystical writer with that of being the mother of a large family. She was very attentive to the needs of her natural and her spiritual children. One of her sons gave this testimony: "What was so awesome in the life of my mother was her natural and simple existence."

Mystical writer

In her autobiography Conchita wrote, "I always had an inclination to writing. It was necessary for my soul to empty itself on paper."[4] In fact, she received a special gift from Jesus for writing her spiritual message. She wrote a great deal in her life. Her published works reach to the number of forty-six, some of them very simple, yet all as a help for meditation and prayer. They amount to approximately nine thousand pages, but these are only an eighth part of her total output. Her unpublished works are even more numerous. These include the 6,227 letters addressed to her spiritual directors which have been preserved, and which are characterized by a high degree of spirituality. Her *Account of Conscience* runs to sixty-six volumes (22,500 pages) and it was written as a sort of account of conscience for her various directors. Besides these, there are various other writings which amount to 15,500 pages.

It is not an easy task to summarize her rich doctrine in a few words, because there is no facet of the mystery of Christ which would not be rather amply developed in her writings and all subjects form a harmonious whole in her Spirituality of the Cross.

Historical background – Mexico, 1928

Conchita's life can be fully understood only in the broader context of modern Mexican history. In her book written at the age of seventeen, *History of a Very Peaceful Family*, she described a tranquil life which her family lived in the *haciendas*. Conchita would never have imagined that the seventy-five years of her life would coincide with the most severe persecution of the Church in Mexico: from the victory of the Juarez party (1861) until General Ávila Camacho became president (1940). The peaceful milieu of the cities and estates of Mexico was thrown into turmoil by the great social changes introduced by the liberal Constitution (1857) and religious persecution. During several of these years the celebration of all religious services was legally prohibited. During the presidency of General Plutarco Elías Calles (1924-1928), the persecution of Catholics in Mexico reached an unprecedented level. In spite of assurances from the Mexican episcopate that the Church was seeking a peaceful and legal approach to constitutional reform, President Calles and his government embarked on a concerted effort to suppress the Catholic Church, beginning in the summer of 1926, with the curtailment of Catholic public worship, the closing of Catholic schools, and the exiling of foreign Catholic priests and bishops. In 1928 the Congress named Emilio Portes Gil (1928-1930) as interim president. The famous rebellion of the Cristeros (an armed movement of Mexican Catholics who were involved in the religious conflict in 1926-1929) sprang up and in some areas became violent. In retaliation, the government initiated even more harsh anticlerical measures, and the Church was forced to suspend all public religious services.

The spiritual retreat recorded in this volume took place during this political and social turmoil. Conchita suffered with the persecuted Church and offered many prayers and sacrifices for it. Providence rewarded her with prophetic "lights" on the meaning of the persecution within the Holy Spirit's universal call to holiness. The suffering which marked the history of Mexico's faithful was revealed to Conchita as a moment of grace for Mexico and the background of the Spirituality of the Cross.

The Spiritual Exercises

The Venerable Concepción Cabrera consistently sought the help of enlightened spiritual directors. During her entire spiritual journey she was guided by gifted directors: Father Alberto Cuscó y Mir, S.J., (1893-1903), Father Felix of Jesus Rougier (1903-1904; 1914-1938), Archbishop Ramón Ibarra y González (1912-1917), Bishop Emeterio Valverde (1917-1925) and Archbishop Luis M. Martínez[5] (1925-1937), as well as many others.

Seeking closer union with God, Conchita used to make a directed retreat (spiritual exercises) every year. During her life she made fifty-four retreats, eleven of these (1925-1936) with Archbishop Luis M. Martínez.[6] Under his direction, Conchita came to understand to an ever greater extent the graces she had already received, became open to receive subsequent ones and eventually prepared herself for her encounter with God (1937).

From the beginning of his spiritual direction (Letter, November 28, 1923), Bishop Martínez encouraged Conchita "to believe with absolute firmness in God's graces." On August 15, 1925, Conchita wrote in her letter to Bishop Martínez: "I feel that I am understood, that you can read me, that I am guided. I really see that God has been preparing you for me. I had begged for a director for so long! How much light, and how it radiates and penetrates into my poor and dark soul."

In the course of the years of his direction Archbishop Martínez came to recognize the spiritual and doctrinal depth of Conchita's reflections. From reading her writings, Bishop Martínez was able to guide her, taking into account the spiritual graces which she had already received and explaining to her the further degrees to which she could aspire. In fact, the written meditations which Bishop Martínez offered to Conchita were on many occasions based on her own writings, which he then explained with his fine theological knowledge. His pastoral gifts enabled him to apply the spiritual themes he offered to Conchita for reflection to a very personal level. These retreats were thus for Conchita an experience which engaged her whole person. Her written insights in response to his were never mere abstractions, but arose from her personal experience with God.

The Retreat of 1928

United with Christ, Conchita shared in His mediation on behalf of the Church. She participated in the priestly sacrifice of Christ on behalf of the Church and humanity, as every baptized person is called to do. This baptismal priesthood is one of the principal subjects of her spirituality. Enlightened by many texts from Conchita's writings, Bishop Martínez chose as the subject for the retreat: "To be Jesus Crucified," which he divided into two parts: (1) "To be Jesus" and (2) "To be Jesus Crucified," since this was God's design for her. Conchita became more fully aware that she belonged to the Church and that her mission was to pray for priests and to be their spiritual mother. Above all, she had to become aware of the priestly role of her own baptism and the necessity of living it fully. It is interesting to observe how the bishop and Conchita became increasingly more aware that the Lord united their mission on behalf of the Church. In his *Intimate Notes*[7] the bishop wrote: "Before I believed that God had united our souls so that we could do much good, but now I see that the union of souls supposes the union of mission."

We can grasp these designs on the part of God expressed in one of the bishop's letters (October 17, 1927): "In the morning, I was reviewing the vows which I made a month ago.... I kissed my crucifix before going to rest, and I held it tight to my heart. This dominant longing came from the depths of my soul: 'I want to be filled with Jesus.' But interiorly, someone added: 'Crucified.' A very clear light filled my spirit and a divine sentiment filled my heart. The beauty, the ineffable beauty of Jesus Crucified, was revealed to me and enraptured my heart.... Kissing the crucifix and holding it tightly to my heart I told Him: 'You are *my* Jesus. Finally I have found You.'"

Conchita answered this letter on October 29, 1927: "Oh what a beautiful subject for your retreat: *To be Jesus Crucified*! What lights on that priestly Heart, which undoubtedly will fuse your heart with His. Have pity; don't leave me out. This is how I conceive a perfect priest, the quintessence of the priesthood, as you used to say. Become like this, and form others to be so, since Jesus desires it so much. Ought we not to give thanks to God for so many graces and lights on the goal of the Works of the Cross, on the mystical priesthood whose seal they carry? You will do great good to them. I don't get tired of blessing the Lord, who gave us the gift of your presence for His Work."

In that retreat, the Lord revealed to Conchita His plan for the Church of Morelia. The culmination of her life and of the Works was to be her loving offering on behalf of priests and the Church. She made that "offering" on the last day of her retreat. She received "the intimate Cross of the Heart of Jesus which is priestly in itself, because it was formed by the very pure substance of priestly love. When this love gets in contact with the sins of the world, it becomes an immense priestly suffering."[8] One of the supreme degrees of charity is to offer this suffering on behalf of those who cause it, as Jesus did it.

The "lived theology" of the saints

Along with so many other mystics in the course of the Church's life, Conchita also illustrated the mystery of Christ from her own unique experience. As we contemplate her spiritual journey, we will perceive an outline of her "Christology."

In his Apostolic Letter *Novo Millennio Ineunte*, John Paul II underscored the importance of what he calls the "science of love." "Faced with this mystery, we are greatly helped not only by theological investigation, but also by that great heritage which is *the 'lived theology' of the saints.* The saints offer us pre[illegible]sights which enable us to understand more easily the intuition of faith thanks to the special enlightenment which some of them have received from the Holy Spirit. Not infrequently, the saints have undergone *something akin to Jesus' experience on the Cross* in the paradoxical blending of bliss and pain. What an illuminating testimony!" (n. 27) … "Is it not one of the 'signs of the times' that in today's world, despite widespread secularization, there is *a widespread demand for spirituality,* a demand which expresses itself in large part as *a renewed need for prayer*?" … "Love is truly the 'heart' of the Church, as was well understood by Saint Thérèse of Lisieux, whom I proclaimed a Doctor of the Church precisely because she is an expert in the *scientia amoris*" (n. 33).

"This science is *mystical theology,*" according to St. John of the Cross, "which is the secret science of God, and which spiritual men call contemplation. It is most full of sweetness because it is *knowledge by love*, love is the master of it, and it is love that renders it all so sweet. Inasmuch as this science and knowledge are communicated to the soul in that love with which God communicates Himself, it is sweet to the understanding, because knowledge belongs to it, and sweet to the will, because it comes by love, which belongs to the will."[9]

From her youth, Conchita wanted to learn how to love Jesus: "When I was eleven years old I thirsted to love something infinite which could satisfy the aspiration of my soul, an emptiness which I could never fill and which I always experienced," she wrote in her *Account of Conscience.*[10] Jesus Himself taught her the "science of love." "Jesus wants love" she wrote in 1894.[11] He explained to her how she should love: "Pray and love; sacrifice yourself and love, asleep or awake, here and there, don't do anything other than love; love for those who despise Me." It was hard to learn the demands of divine love. To Jesus' question: "Do you want to love the way you want to or the way I want you to; your way or My way?" She answered: "My Jesus, as You wish, even though my nature may resist." With such an answer, Jesus concluded: "Let

Me fashion you without your least resistance; don't stop My arm; allow Me to work and make of your soul what pleases Me."[12]

During her whole life she tried to live constantly the great commandment of love: "This is heaven on earth: to love Jesus, to love Jesus, and all in Jesus and through Jesus." "I have a very ardent desire for perfection… to love more, to imitate and follow Jesus more… to suffer for Him."[13] The Heart of Jesus is the sacrament of Trinitarian love. In 1895, she understood by a special light of the Holy Spirit: "My Heart is the Heart of Jesus and also that of the Father. We are Three Persons, but with the same Heart, that is, the same love and the same will. Love and make that Heart loved." Toward the end of her life, still pining for perfect joy, she achieved loving with the Holy Spirit, who brought her love to perfection and found His satisfaction and repose in it.[14]

In his *Canticle*, St. John of the Cross underscored Christ's unlimited richness: "Notwithstanding the marvelous mysteries which holy doctors have discovered, and holy souls have understood in this life, many more remain behind. There are in Christ great depths to be fathomed, for He is a rich mine, with many recesses full of treasures, and however deeply we may descend we shall never reach the end, for in every recess new veins of new treasures abound in all directions… But the soul cannot reach these hidden treasures unless it first passes through the thicket of interior and exterior suffering: for even such knowledge of the mysteries of Christ as is possible in this life cannot be had without great sufferings, and without many intellectual and moral gifts, and without previous spiritual exercises; for all these gifts are far inferior to this knowledge of the mysteries of Christ, being only a preparation for it."[15]

The unfathomable "science of love" is at the same time the "science of suffering." Conchita quickly came to understand that love must be united with suffering: "I want to love you, Jesus, with fire, with vehemence, with overwhelming passion, even if it means Calvary for me." Yet the particular nuance of suffering, characteristic of her spirituality was the "interior cross of the Heart of Jesus," that is, the interior sufferings of Jesus for the Cl Archbishop Martínez explained to her: "to love as suffer as He suffers, to drink the same chalice of bitterness which He drank. This is accomplished in an ineffable way when you share in the intimate suffering of Jesus."[16]

The Trinitarian aspect

In her spiritual experience, the Venerable Concepción encountered the triune God. In the vision of the Cross of the Apostolate she became aware that the Father, the Son and the Holy Spirit made themselves present in her life: "The Cross of the Apostolate encompasses the principal mysteries of our faith: the mystery of the Blessed Trinity is represented there in this way: the light which bathes the Cross represents the Eternal Father; the light which radiates from the Cross signifies Jesus, the Incarnate Son of God; the other light, which radiates and spreads out from the Dove, represents the Holy Spirit. The august mystery of the Blessed Trinity is represented there: three lights in one sole light… three virtues in the same Divinity, three components in the one same God. Blessed is he who attains to penetrating into this simultaneous unity! Jesus showed her the path 'to glorify the Trinity in heaven by doing its will on earth.'"[17]

The Eucharist opened up before her the unknown horizons of unity in the Trinity: "After my communion I *felt* – because you cannot understand it with human understanding – that Jesus, the second Person of the Blessed Trinity, is within God, and God, the Father and the Holy Spirit within Him. They are different Persons in one sole divine substance…. The Three Persons form the very same substance, and this substance is the Divinity, it is God. When they communicate themselves to the soul through this Sacrament, they communicate the same divine substance to it. This communication is so intimate that it transforms the soul into God's own substance, if the soul has the proper dispositions. By means of this Sacrament the soul is divinized and tends to

God, who is its center. The soul becomes one with Him just as two flames together form one, without being separate. The world does not penetrate to the heights of this mystery of love, does not understand its great value, since it encompasses nothing less than the most perfect *union* of the soul with God."[18]

God's love which is diffused is the Trinitarian love, love which saves and returns to man his lost dignity. The Trinity communicates its love in its works: "The very substance of the Father is love, and so great on man's behalf that He gave His own Son for Redemption. The substance of the Son is love, and this love is so great for the Father and for man that He handed Himself over to save him and thus to honor His Father. The substance of the Holy Spirit is love which acts together with the Father and the Son for the glory of the Trinity, thus participating in the mystery of the Incarnation. The Holy Spirit was present in the life of Jesus testifying to His divinity, sealing the work of the Redemption and protecting the Church, His immaculate Spouse. The substance of the Father is love and power. The substance of the Holy Spirit is love and life. The substance of the Son is love and suffering. The substance of the Three Persons of the Trinity is charity, that is, the very pure love of communication which for this reason is called charity, because it is communicated and is the most perfect love of charity."[19]

The Father

The Person of the Father, after the Person of Jesus, has a privileged place in Conchita's writings. The word appears 13,428 times in her *Account of Conscience*, without counting published works. One finds, for example, reference to the Father in His relation to the Trinity; the Father in His relation with Jesus as the preexistent Word and Redeemer; the Father in relation to the Incarnation and Mary; the Father, creation, human beings and sin; the Father and the Church, sacraments and virtues; the Father, the Cross and the meaning of suffering; the Father and priests.

Jesus taught Conchita filial love for the Father: [illegible]
to invoke the Father who is My Father and yours. Ca[illegible]
with filial love, which pleases Him so much. His role is that of the authority between us. Entreat Him, entreat Him a lot and with great confidence. Call upon Him: 'Father, Father!' When desolation or any other kind of sorrow afflicts you, when you are exhausted and I hide Myself from you, and your little Dove hides too, cry out to Him imitating Me, and say to Him: 'Father, into Your hands I commend My spirit!' Place all in His loving hands. Where better will you be able to rest? Who will be able to take care of you with tenderness like His? You cannot imagine how much He appreciates a crucified soul." Jesus is the Mediator of all graces: "I, I am He who gives value to all acts in heaven and on earth; only through Me is the Father glorified; I am the Head and those who belong to Me are My own Body."[20]

Jesus wanted to share with Conchita His profound redemptive desires: "I'm hungry, hungry for pure victim souls, self-sacrificing souls who will placate My Father's justice. I want the earth to burn with the wood of the cross and the fire of the Holy Spirit. I want these souls to pray for My Church. I want *holy priests*, so that they may work for My glory and not for theirs.... I want love, I thirst for love, consolation and reparation in the Eucharist.... Give Me souls, give Me crucified hearts, give Me your whole heart that I may fill and possess it...." Jesus wanted her "to do His Father's will in all things."[21]

Conchita was invited to establish a deep union with Jesus: "As I am in My Father and I am one with Him, so I want you to be one with Me. I want you to be like a very pure mirror where the image of your *Jesus Crucified* can be reproduced: just as I am on the Cross, so I want to reflect Myself in you; only offer yourself to receive My image; and I want you to be like Me: crowned, flogged, desolate, pierced, abandoned.... Meditate one by one on all these things and be My living portrait in order that My Father may be pleased with you and pour out graces on sinners."[22] Jesus came "to bring fire on earth, so that it might consume the wickedness of hearts and thus purify them and dispose them to His Father."[23]

Like Mary, Conchita had to learn the difficult love which crucified Jesus as His Father had done: "My Father loved Me as He loved no one else… His love for Me is above all love… and nevertheless, *He crucified Me….* Mary's role is to crucify Me, to offer Me in holocaust, and this will be your role…."[24] Living for the glory of the Father, Conchita had to offer her life and sacrifices to the Father in union with Jesus for the salvation of souls.

This brief "Introduction" does not allow one to study all the nuances of the rich doctrine of Conchita on the Father. She bequeathed to the Works of the Cross the duty of honoring the Father with filial love, calling upon Him often and keeping the members of the Works very pure in order to reflect the image of Divinity in them.[25]

The Holy Spirit

In the *Account of Conscience* of the Venerable Concepción Cabrera de Armida the theme of the Holy Spirit appears 4,233 times, with its variants "young dove" (*palomita*) or "young pigeon" (*pichoncito*) 985 times, as she liked to call Him with familiar tenderness. She developed the following subjects at length: the being of the Holy Spirit; the Holy Spirit in relation with Jesus; the Holy Spirit in the Incarnation of the Word and in relation with Mary; the sanctifying role of the Holy Spirit; the Holy Spirit and the Church: sin, grace, prayer, virtues, gifts, fruits and sacraments; the Holy Spirit, the Cross and the priests; the Reign of the Holy Spirit; to love with the Holy Spirit; the fruitfulness of the Holy Spirit and the "third love." Conchita never lived the mystery of the Divine Persons separately, but she always contemplated the deep union existing between them.

The "nest" of the Holy Spirit

With the symbolism of the Cross of the Apostolate, Conchita understood that the Heart of Jesus was a sacrament of Trinitarian love, a real "nest" of the Holy Spirit. She was invited to be a nest of the Holy Spirit, in imitation of Jesus: "You cannot understand this immense favor of being a *nest of the Holy Spirit*, of the Spirit of the Father and the Son...." The Holy Spirit "hovers over this arid valley of earth," Conchita wrote in 1895, "and does not find a place to rest and make His nest since where He does not find the Heart of Jesus, His nest par excellence, He only alights momentarily, but does not settle, or repose, or nest. In short, He needs crucified souls...."[26]

By means of this modest symbol, which forms part of the rich symbolical network in Conchita's writings, she tried to express a profound reality, namely that the Holy Spirit always dwells "in the Heart of Jesus, in the adorable Eucharist, in the purest breast of Mary, since these three places form only one, the selfsame nest," because nobody can reach Him except through the God-Man.[27]

As the Holy Spirit is the Creator Spirit: "He makes everything fruitful with His purest breath" and "forms in His nests holy spirits, feeding them with all the virtues, gifts and fruits... the grace flows from Him, making souls fruitful for heaven." Conchita began to be His nest "from the moment she started to be His Cross. His nests form crosses and His crosses form His nests, which always have the form of a cross." The Holy Spirit formed the heart of Conchita through her practice of virtues, because "in the perfection of the virtues there is a real transformation into Jesus."[28] Souls that follow "the spirit of the Cross" are highly favored by Him.

Conchita had to guard her nest because "it has three mortal enemies: *the world*, *vanity* and *pride*. When these enemies touch His nests, the Holy Spirit detests them, leaves and sometimes does not return." She understood that she "had to hide Him from all human gazes, except from her spiritual director. He normally speaks and communicates Himself in interior solitude; He fills what He finds *empty* and illumines what is *dark*. He wants His crosses to become nests, *emptied* of the world and of self, *hidden* in solitude, and *in darkness* from all that is not Himself." These are the necessary dispositions "to listen to the Holy Spirit's groanings, which make heaven tremble for their delicacy… and which cause the eternal happiness of the Father and the Son."[29]

For me to live is Christ

To speak of the presence of Christ in Conchita's writings would not suffice, since Christ became the essence of her life: "Life consists in the sequence of instants; then my instants are Christ; I owe them to Him. He is the sacred source from which life and love constantly flow. He is my sustenance, my breath, my life.… I feel like this, my Jesus: my desire is Your desire; where You go, I go; where You are, I am there."[30]

She understood that the constant imitation of Christ was necessary: "But during Your life, my Jesus, You only saw the cross…. You only heard calumny, disdain and ingratitude…. You only tasted bile and vinegar. You only felt beatings, weariness, cold, hunger, thirst and unspeakable torments…. You were only a Man of suffering…." Her contemplation of the redemptive suffering of Christ made her desire: "to be disdained, forsaken, detested and hidden in Christ."[31]

As a mother and wife, Conchita had many obligations, but her great desire was to be in a convent. Jesus opened to her His Heart, which would become her cloister: "Now you really live in Me… and within Me and I will be your atmosphere; you will inhale and exhale Christ, your Spouse. Your soul will never be able to break this grate, but your thought will soar all over the world, because it is like this while you live in this world. Nonetheless, I want to purify this. Try to think *within your Jesus*. Meditate well on these words and put them into practice. You should not only live, but also think and feel within your Jesus, inside your Cloister and close to Mary." Conchita, fascinated by this divine solution, responded: "I will annihilate and hide myself, become fused into my Christ. I will get lost in Him so that I will never find myself and if so, only to humiliate myself."[32]

She understood that "in the solitude of her heart" she was the spouse of the Crucified: "I will occupy myself only with my *Christ Crucified*... with His Cross."[33] The Cross of the Apostolate[34] became her spiritual path. In 1887, Jesus explained to her: "This Cross is the edifice of perfection: all mysteries are represented in it... the gifts and the fruits of the Holy Spirit; the three theological virtues are represented in the Blessed Trinity that is presented there; and the *Path* which Jesus presents is in His Divine Heart on the Cross." This Cross "snatches hearts from the earth."[35] Thus the Cross of Christ not only depicts the negative sign of sin, but also the sign of the highest manifestation of Trinitarian love.

Jesus required many purifications of her, because He wanted her soul to be "very pure... and clean, more than the crystal of a mirror, unstained, without deceit and wrinkle, so that He might paint His blessed image on it." Surprised by Jesus' invitation, Conchita asked how she could: "Paint Christ in her heart!" The answer was that she should use "the fine paintbrush of the virtues."[36] Transformation into Christ has an interior dynamism: "In the process of transformation there are many degrees as in virtues, and to the extent of the soul's likeness with Jesus, the Eternal Father possesses, loves and elevates it. He is pleased with it because of its likeness to His Incarnate Word, whom He loves most."[37]

The Virgin of Solitude was her model and the inseparable companion on her journey: "The Passion of Jesus was also the Passion of Mary. Mary was full of grace, love and sorrow." Being very realistic, Conchita recognized: "Ah, my God! How much it costs vile human nature to belong to Jesus, to live by Him...." She didn't let worries get her down: "Love drew Christ to the sacrifice and the same love will draw Concepción so that He may be pleased with her...."[38] Jesus absorbed her entire person. He was the supreme model of her spiritual path and the mediator of her union with the Triune God.

"The Cross of Jesus"

The centrality of the Cross in Conchita's spiritual life was cultivated in the crucible of the great transforming sorrows of life.

Christ without the Cross does not exist and to speak about Christ means to speak about Christ "Crucified." We Christians are the followers of Christ Crucified. Being followers of Christ means being marked by His Cross. In the history of salvation many chosen souls received a new name which defined their new mission. Jesus gave Conchita a new name which marked her vocation: "You are My Cross, and I want you to be thus named and I want you to sign yourself as *Cross of Jesus*." From the moment of His spousal covenant with Conchita, Jesus also gave Himself a new name, that is, "*Jesus of My Cross*."[39] In order to help Conchita to accomplish her mission contained in her new name, Jesus led her progressively. The first symbolic circumstance was a corpus of Christ which she bought that did not have a cross. Jesus told her: "Don't put it on a cross because you are His cross."[40] She used to carry this corpus without a cross: "For years I used to wear that corpus on my chest without a cross. I never wanted to put it on a cross because, so to speak, *I was His cross*."[41]

Conchita learned to suffer lovingly as Jesus explained to her: "The mistake consists in this: that everybody thinks that there is only suffering on the Cross. Those who say this don't really love; love is satisfied precisely in suffering; in suffering for one whom we love, we find happiness in all its extensions." The Crucified Spouse identified her with Himself: "You are My Cross, My beloved Cross, the insignia of love, the nest of the Spouse."[42] Jesus used to joke with her, playing on words: "You are My shell Cross and I will rest on My Cross."[43]

"Jesus, Savior of mankind..."

Among so many lights in Conchita's *Account of Conscience* on the mystery of God, the Church, the priesthood, the mission of lay people, etc., the references to Jesus Christ are the most abundant and amount to 25,393. There is a real, rich and original Christology in her Spirituality of the Cross.

Conchita was called to be a consolation to the Heart of Jesus in the name of the whole human race if she corresponded to His love. Already in 1889, she understood that "her mission was to save souls."[44] At that time the full dimensions of her vocation had not yet clearly emerged, but she noted: "...my whole longing was to belong totally to Jesus by all possible means within my reach. I had permission for corporal penances, but they were far away from quenching my thirst for suffering, which rather grew and grew ever more passionate. In those days, I began to make my night-prayer lying on a cross made of thorns which would cover my whole back. Hair shirts, whips, prayer during the night, nothing, no mortification was able to moderate that fire which devoured me. Many times I asked my spiritual director permission to engrave the Holy Name of Jesus on my chest, and he did not want to grant it to me."

Finally, on January 14, 1894, the feast of the Holy Name of Jesus, Conchita was able to accomplish this symbolic gesture of total belonging to Jesus. Once the Name of Jesus was branded on her chest with the red-hot iron, she experienced an even more ardent desire for the salvation of souls: "I had the impression of forgetting myself because a new great and extraordinary sentiment overwhelmed me and made me cry out: 'Jesus, Jesus, Savior of mankind, save them, save them!'"[45] The Lord was pleased with that act of love and one morning when she was in prayer she "saw Him open the clothes on His chest and show her, smiling, a wound like hers... she could read her name in that wound on the holy chest of the Lord."[46]

The monogram was an occasion for the Lord to bestow new

graces which would extend to the Church and the world. Conchita wrote: "It seemed that through the monogram the Lord opened a door to pour Himself out in graces."[47] The Holy Spirit granted her the grace of zeal for the salvation of souls, which would be carried out by means of the Works of the Cross and the Spirituality of the Cross.

Within the Heart of Jesus

The zealous cry "Jesus, Savior of mankind, save them" which sprang from her heart "was her martyrdom and happiness." Conchita had to become a living Cross of the Apostolate, that is, reflect in herself and be thoroughly penetrated with the mystery of salvation. The growing zeal for the salvation of souls and the spiritual path revealed to her in the Cross of the Apostolate led her into the depth of the mystery of redemption. Jesus wanted the interior Cross of His Heart to be known and invited her to participate in it: "The Cross which pierces My Heart symbolizes the interior Cross which I had from the first moment of My Incarnation in the womb of My Mother. Both crosses are precious and the exterior one will draw souls to the interior one which is known only by very few."[48]

As the spiritual mother of the Works of the Cross, Conchita lived the gift of the interior passion of Jesus: "I was nailed to the Cross on Calvary for only three hours, but I was nailed to that of My Heart My entire life; both of them will be honored in the Oasis,[49] but particularly the interior one which represents My interior, incomprehensible pain and suffering which kept My soul oppressed… those sufferings were hidden even during My hidden life. My external passion lasted only some hours and was like a dew, a solace for the other cruel passion which I carried within My soul."[50]

Guided by Mary, Conchita tried to enter into the Heart of Jesus in every communion and to taste its bitterness caused by the ingratitude of men. She eventually arrived at the very hidden, interior cross, the very essence of the Heart of Jesus. "This cross is sweet, no matter how bitter it may be, it is suave in spite of its roughness, it is the treasure and repose of those souls, it is perfection on earth," according to Jesus' explanations.

Conchita perpetuated the interior passion of Jesus, sharing in the interior sufferings of His Heart in order to console Him. United with Him, she participated in His redemptive work on behalf of souls. Jesus asked for this: "Don't leave Me alone, don't go, make acts of reparation, console Me. I want you to accompany Me in the Garden.... Look, on My Way of the Cross many accompanied Me, then on Calvary some souls, but in My desolation in the Garden almost nobody; most fell asleep. I want you close to Me. I fought with demons and you will fight; I suffered a terrible interior martyrdom and you will suffer it... in that place there was no cross, no thorns, no lashes nor material nails and, nonetheless, My Heart experienced all their torments. My hidden martyrdom was thousands of times worse than the visible one on the Cross. Yours will be like this...."[51]

The following and imitation of Christ have particular connotations for Conchita. She will imitate Him "in the interior, sorrowful and hidden life in the depth of His Heart; the life consumed by desolation, struggles and abandonment; the life of sacrifice, pierced and crucified... the life made bitter with all the bitterness of the spirit... the life of the interior cross, but perfect, hidden from all human gazes... the life which destroys the soul, purifying it in darkness and silence." In these circumstances, Conchita used to repeat the short prayer: "Jesus, allow me to experience the suffering which every offense that You receive causes to Your Heart, because I want to accompany You," offering acts of atonement.[52]

To be Jesus Crucified

Considering the spiritual journey of Conchita, we can speak of a period before her central grace, the mystical incarnation

(March 25, 1906), and a period after it. The Lord prepared her for this grace in the course of nine years which included other very special graces like betrothal, spiritual marriage (1897), lights on the mystery of the Trinity, the Church and many others.

The mystical incarnation was for her a powerful transforming grace, which simplified and unified her life, profoundly identifying her with her Model, Jesus, the "Man of sorrows."[53] Eminently Christocentric, this grace submerged and involved Conchita in the salvific dynamism of the Incarnation of the Word, since it is impossible to separate the Incarnation from its redemptive finality. Since the Trinity manifests itself and is always at work, Christocentrism consequently implies Trinitarian dynamism.

This Trinitarian grace includes a special outpouring of the Holy Spirit, an intimate union with the Word, and originates in the fruitful gaze of the Heavenly Father. The ineffable divine operations are continuous, not occasional, simple and eternal. The soul united to the Holy Spirit in pure and profound love receives from Him the fruitfulness of the Father and "becomes Jesus" in order to share in an ineffable way in His priesthood, exercising this priesthood fruitfully on behalf of souls, especially on behalf of priests. It is essentially a transformation into Jesus, Priest and Victim.[54]

By means of the mystical incarnation, Conchita was transformed into Christ and shared in His redemptive work in a more perfect way than before. This grace has many degrees, but basically we can distinguish three aspects in it: (1) the aspect of being priest and victim, (2) the Eucharistic aspect, and (3) the Marian aspect.

(1) Regarding the *aspect of being priest and victim*, we find the fundamental nucleus of the entire co-redeeming dynamism which the grace of the mystical incarnation developed in Conchita. She learned to offer the Word to the Eternal Father and to offer herself in union with Him for the redemption of the world. Her intercession acquired a fundamental value based upon her

possession of the Divine Victim of Calvary, the Eucharist within herself.

The nuance of oblation which the grace acquired in her, since Jesus became mystically incarnate in her, enabled her in a certain sense to imitate the Father's love. Consequently, she could offer Jesus and offer herself in union with Him in the same way that His Mother did. Conchita had to identify her will with that of the Father, who allowed His Son to be crucified. This mission was neatly synthesized by the Lord: "offer Me and offer yourself, this at every instant, with the purpose of saving souls and giving glory to the Father."

(2) The grace of the mystical incarnation led Conchita to live the life of Jesus in such a way that her body was mystically identified with Jesus' Body and her blood with His Blood, because Jesus, mystically incarnate in her heart, had the power to transform her and unite her to His immolation. This *aspect of offering acquired a Eucharistic connotation*. In offering herself, Conchita had not only to be assimilated to the Incarnate Word, but she also had to be transformed into Him. This is why, by the realization of a sort of transubstantiation into Jesus, Conchita could truly say: "This is my Body; this is my Blood,"[55] because it was no longer she who lived, but Christ who lived in her (cf. Gal 2:20).

According to the teaching of the Second Vatican Council, the baptismal character gives us the capacity to offer Christ and to offer ourselves in union with Him, but it is precisely in the Eucharist that a Christian is fully transformed into Christ and brings to fulfillment His priestly offering. Conchita lived the Mass in a mystically continuous way, prolonging in her heart and in her life the "offertory" and the "consecration."[56] That Mass was perpetuated through the practice called the "Chain of Love," which consists in "offering Christ and offering oneself in union with Him at every moment of one's life and in the practice of the virtues." She fully lived her baptismal priesthood.

(3) Regarding the *Marian aspect*, Conchita contemplated

Mary as the model of collaborating in the work of redemption. Mary taught her to live this priestly and Eucharistic dynamism with a maternal heart. Conchita had to reflect the life of Mary and be a faithful echo of her maternal heart, with the same purpose: for the glory of the Father and the salvation of souls.[57] The maternal mediation of Conchita was always and only "mediation in Christ," after the pattern of Mary's maternal mediation.

Like Mary and with her, Conchita was not only to be a mother of Jesus by virtue of the mystical incarnation, but also a mother of His Mystical Body, the Church. This participation in the redeeming offering of Jesus acquired thus the nuance of ecclesial maternity. Like Mary, she received the grace to be spiritually present in all Eucharistic celebrations. Mary taught her to live her baptismal priesthood in a maternal way.[58] This stage of the life of Mary, Mother of the Church, Conchita called the "stage of the solitude of Mary," and it extended from the Ascension of Jesus until her Assumption. In the years of her solitude, Mary lived her maternal priesthood in perfect joy. Conchita lived the same experience of Mary, being the echo of her Heart; she accepted her maternal martyrdom of love on behalf of others.

The role of the Trinity, particularly of the Holy Spirit, should be underlined in the dynamism of this grace, since the mystical incarnation is accomplished by the Holy Spirit and leads to a deeper union with Him. Jesus explained it to Conchita: "The mystical incarnation of the Word attracts the Holy Spirit who accomplished it in the soul with the eternal fruitfulness of the Father and He does not separate Himself from it, taking care of it and protecting the Divine Word, Jesus, whose spirit is the same Holy Spirit. Therefore, when the transformation of the soul into Jesus takes place – the mystical incarnation is to help in this – the Holy Spirit also becomes the spirit of the creature, to a greater or lesser degree, according to the intensity and degree of the transformation, which depends very much on the correspondence of the soul in the virtues. Then, the Holy Spirit, absorbing the spirit of the creature in its transformation, fills it with that most pure love which is Himself and then with that same love, the creature loves the Divine Word, that is, with the love itself with which the Father loves Him and is loved, with the perfection of love."[59]

Conchita learned to love Jesus and the Father through the action of the Holy Spirit. The perfect interior life, which is the crowning of the mystical incarnation, is attained when the soul occupies itself only in glorifying the Father, in consuming all its energies, desires and love in only one will and love, in the Holy Spirit; when it offers itself to the Father in union with the Word as a victim of perennial expiation, only to give Him glory.[60]

On behalf of the Church

The grace of the mystical incarnation is multiple in its effects for others. The Church and the sanctification of priests were always at the center of Conchita's prayers. The grace which originated in the gaze of the Father in 1894 culminated in the full transformation into Christ for the glory of the Father and the salvation of souls. The grace of the mystical incarnation and the baptismal priesthood are deeply related. The Lord wanted to teach Christians to live in communion with Him by being united in the same offering for the same purpose. Thus, the unity of the Mystical Body is realized. Conchita's mission is to promote in the Church the participation in the spiritual priesthood of the one Priest and Mediator, Jesus Christ.

On the Cross Conchita found perfect joy, because she attained to perfect union with Christ. At the twilight of her life, Conchita complained that she was experiencing complete abandonment, as if she had never known Jesus, but she abandoned herself trustfully to "God who abandoned her." She wrote: "Oh my Jesus, if I could truly say with You '*Consummatum est*' at the hour of my death, I would be so happy! Will You grant it to me? Yet this will be accomplished when I will be nailed on my definitive cross, when no part of my being will be able to escape from the influence of suffering… and my heart will be a reflection of

Yours."[61] Those who were present at the moment of Conchita's last agony were very impressed by the aspect of her body, which resembled that of Jesus on the Cross. Her name "*Cross of Jesus*," was engraved on her tombstone.

Sr. Elzbieta Sadowska, RCSCJ
Msgr. Arthur B. Calkins

Biblical Abbreviations

OLD TESTAMENT

Genesis	Gn	Nehemiah	Ne	Baruch	Ba
Exodus	Ex	Tobit	Tb	Ezekiel	Ezk
Leviticus	Lv	Judith	Jdt	Daniel	Dn
Numbers	Nb	Esther	Est	Hosea	Ho
Deuteronomy	Dt	1 Maccabees	1 M	Joel	Jl
Joshua	Jos	2 Maccabees	2 M	Amos	Am
Judges	Jg	Job	Jb	Obadiah	Ob
Ruth	Rt	Psalms	Ps	Jonah	Jon
1 Samuel	1 S	Proverbs	Pr	Micah	Mi
2 Samuel	2 S	Ecclesiastes	Ec	Nahum	Na
1 Kings	1 K	Song of Songs	Sg	Habakkuk	Hab
2 Kings	2 K	Wisdom	Ws	Zephaniah	Zp
1 Chronicles	1 Ch	Sirach	Si	Haggai	Hg
2 Chronicles	2 Ch	Isaiah	Is	Malachi	Ml
Ezra	Ezr	Jeremiah	Jr	Zechariah	Zc
		Lamentations	Lm		

NEW TESTAMENT

Matthew	Mt	Ephesians	Eph	Hebrews	Heb
Mark	Mk	Philippians	Ph	James	Jm
Luke	Lk	Colossians	Col	1 Peter	1 P
John	Jn	1 Thessalonians	1 Th	2 Peter	2 P
Acts	Ac	2 Thessalonians	2 Th	1 John	1 Jn
Romans	Rm	1 Timothy	1 Tm	2 John	2 Jn
1 Corinthians	1 Cor	2 Timothy	2 Tm	3 John	3 Jn
2 Corinthians	2 Cor	Titus	Tt	Jude	Jude
Galatians	Gal	Philemon	Phm	Revelation	Rv

Retreat Directed by Archbishop Luis M. Martínez

Morelia, Mexico, 1928

Morelia, November 21, 1928

Yesterday I arrived in this beloved city of the Sacred Heart.[62] Lolita Buitrón[63] was waiting for me. There I received Communion. I was hungry for Jesus!

I was received very politely. I had lunch with them and in the afternoon I came to this house associated with so many memories of last year's retreat.

I arrived at the house close to the Bishop's residence[64] and I was happy to greet him.

We had dinner together. The Bishop spoke about God for a while and we recollected ourselves in prayer.

We spoke at length about my soul. He has always been so good to me, giving me his precious time!

Thank you, my God. May I benefit from this holy spiritual direction for Your greater glory.

Morelia, November 22, 1928

This morning I offered Mass and Communion that my retreat might bear much fruit. The Bishop offered Mass for the same intention.

As I had already mentioned, we had already spoken much about God, and at 4 p.m. I had already made a preparatory meditation, which I repeated at 6 p.m.

I dedicate this holy retreat to the Holy Spirit, through the hands of the Immaculate Virgin Mary.

Help me, Most Holy Trinity, so that these days may glorify You and redound to Your greater glory.

Preparatory Talk of Bishop Martínez

TO BE JESUS CRUCIFIED

This will be the subject of your retreat, because it is God's ideal for your soul. In the course of your life God has bestowed wonderful graces on you. Who could count them? Who could measure them? Who could appreciate them? Some of these graces you already know, others will be revealed to you in eternity.

What is God's intention in lavishing these graces upon you? What is He waiting for? What does He want? To see Jesus Crucified in your soul with His intimate sentiments, with His divine efficacy, with His holy fruitfulness in glorifying the Heavenly Father.[65]

How much the Lord longs to see His work of mercy and love fulfilled! How much He yearns for this work to be perfect! This work will be a monument to His mercy, the repose of His love and an instrument of His glory.

The more an artist advances in his work, the more enthusiastic he is about it, and so much the more does he desire to finish it. So also the Holy Spirit feels divine enthusiasm and holy impatience – in our way of speaking – to finish His work of love and suffering which consists in the perfect transformation of Concha into Jesus Crucified.

It is for this reason that He brought you to this retreat in order to give a powerful incentive to His work of transformation and perhaps to conclude it.[66]

How solemn, how fruitful, how holy these days seem to me! Your duty and mine is to place ourselves docilely, faithfully and *lovingly* at the disposition of the Holy Spirit.

What can we do but surrender ourselves, allowing the Holy Spirit to possess us, to guide us and to penetrate us?

Consequently, this retreat must begin with a full, total, absolute offering of both of us to the Holy Spirit, through the immaculate hands of Virgin Mary. We will listen to His voice, we will follow His impulses, we will let His fire of love and suffering consume us. In these days we will be *totally His*, *only His*. The loftier and more divine a work is, the less human action avails, and God's action ought to be more intimate, intense and sovereign. In these highest of God's works we have only one task: to offer ourselves without reserve, to be lost in Him and to let ourselves go.

NOVEMBER 23, 1928[67]

FIRST DAY

First Meditation from 6:30 to 7:30 a. m.

Meditation of Archbishop Martínez

We will divide this subject into two sections: to be Jesus and to be Jesus Crucified.[68]

I. TO BE JESUS

You must be Jesus for the Heavenly Father. Jesus is the only one in whom the Father is pleased. Just as all who love want to see the image of the beloved everywhere, so the Father wants to see Jesus reproduced in souls. How many graces He lavishes on you in order to accomplish this loving design! What marvels He has realized in your soul in order to transform you into Jesus!

Your gratitude to the Father, your desire to glorify Him, your longing to show Him your tenderness and your happiness in receiving His luminous, fruitful and tender gaze should encourage you to be Jesus for Him *always* and *in all*. How?

Gazing on the Father through the eyes of Jesus or letting Jesus gaze on Him through your eyes

We can conceive of the mystery of the Trinity in our human way as a loving gaze between the Father and the Son. Jesus, the Word made flesh, lives in the light of the Father's gaze and corresponds to that infinite gaze with the constant, loving gaze of His soul, which seems to be fused with the eternal gaze of the Word.

The core of Jesus' intimate life was this ineffable gaze; His bodily eyes were frequently lifted up to the Father, but the eyes of His soul were always lifted up to Him.

Jesus put all of His soul into that gaze, because that gaze was contemplation, love, self-giving, abandonment, longing to glorify the Father, an abyss of tenderness and a firm, loving, full commitment to His will.

Everything in Jesus had that intimate gaze as its source and it radiated in His physiognomy and was reflected in His words and miracles.

Jesus found traces of the Heavenly Father in all things and through them He saw Him. Above all, He gazed upon the Father in souls, since something divine, the image of the Trinity, shines in souls.

When Jesus looked with love at the young man of whom the Gospel speaks, He looked at the image of the Father in the depth of that pure soul. Just as the sun dispels the mist which covers the earth in order to give its kiss of light to the wild flowers, so when Jesus' gaze converted St. Peter and transformed the Magdalene, the divine efficacy of His gazes dispelled the shadows of sin and the miseries which enshrouded this beloved image in order to find the image of the Father in the depth of these souls.

The gaze of your soul must be the reflection of Jesus' gaze on the Father. This gaze must be the heart of your interior life.

What principally characterizes a physiognomy is the gaze. It is enough to see the eyes of the beloved person in order to recognize him, even if we don't see the features of his face. Thus it seems to me that the Father seeks above all this unique gaze in souls – which delights and pleases Him – in order to know if they are Jesus. It seems to me that the Father is looking for the physiognomy of Jesus in souls and in this physiognomy He seeks above all the gaze of Jesus.

May the Father always find the sweet, pure, adoring and tender gaze of Jesus in your soul.

Look ceaselessly upon the Father with the pure gaze of adoration, self-giving and abandonment; in this gaze put all the virtues and beauty which Jesus used to put in His ineffable gaze, or rather, let Jesus gaze upon the Father through the gaze of your soul.

Gaze upon the Father in the same way on tranquil and sunny days as well as on the gray days when your soul is enshrouded by clouds of sorrow, desolation and abandonment. Gaze upon Him, accompanying your gazes whether of tears or smiles, but gaze upon Him always. The soul's holy gazes, which are raised toward heaven, pierce all shadows and clouds because they are gazes of faith, because they are loving gazes which penetrate heaven's heights.

Don't you think that Jesus' gaze was always tender, sweet and rich; the same on Tabor as it was on Calvary, the same in the Upper Room as it was in Gethsemane?

At times your gaze will be joyful, and at other times sorrowful, but joy and sorrow are essentially love, which can be hidden beneath all veils and clothed in all forms.

Look upon the Father in all creatures: in the splendid heavens, the cheerful meadows, the gigantic mountains, and the immense ocean. Above all, look upon Him in souls, because He is portrayed better in them than in the blue sky and in the waves of the sea. Look upon Him in souls and Jesus will grant to your gaze the wonderful virtue of dispersing the shadows which envelop souls, and He will purify them in order to find the Father's beloved image in them.

But do not forget that Jesus' gaze was first and foremost a priestly gaze: the gaze of the one who loves and offers Himself for the glory of the Father, of the one who implores graces for souls.

Jesus wanted His gaze to be perpetuated by priests. This gaze is raised toward the Father at every moment, since Mass is celebrated at every moment all over the world.

Do you remember all that Jesus said about this gaze? Share mystically in Jesus' priesthood. You should gaze upon the Father with this gaze, since your sacrifice does not have a fixed time as the Eucharistic Sacrifice has, but it is continuous. Your priestly gaze must be constant in order to make up for the imperfect gazes of priests and to be united with the saints.

For the S*econd Meditation*, I simply continued to reflect on the Bishop's words.

Personal Reflection of Conchita

This meditation made me weep many times, since it was so rich, so deep and anointed.

Jesus has been silent.

Finally!

Finally today, unexpectedly, Jesus said to me:

"I brought you here so that you might find rest and strength to continue your life of loving sacrifice on behalf of the Church and especially on behalf of her Shepherds.

"I brought you to console this soul[69] and to pour out My graces on this flock.

"I want to purify your soul more and more in whatever crucible may please Me. I want many things from you."

"But which ones, my Jesus?"

"Some of them you will see, others you will not; but all will be for My Church and for My glory."

"Lord, have You already broken Your silence?"

"I always speak, I am the Word, and I know how to vibrate in souls in many ways."

"Lord, isn't it true that You felt sorry for me? Or why were You so silent?"

"I have My times and besides, you are not always ready. Keep in mind that you are Mine and you are an instrument of My goodness for many."[70]

For the *Third Meditation*, I simply continued to reflect on the Bishop's words.

The *Fourth Meditation* was the following one:

Meditation of Archbishop Martínez

Loving the Father as Jesus Loves Him

Jesus' Heart is all love, only love, always love for His Heavenly Father. His passion for souls is basically His passion for the Father. Love is the origin, center and life of His ineffable sufferings and of His divine virtues.

Who could approach the Heart of Jesus, this abyss of love for the Father? This love is unique, total, everlasting, very pure, selfless, active, tender and self-sacrificing. Each one of these characteristics contains inexhaustible treasures, but it is better to contemplate them with the heart's eyes than to explain them with words.

Jesus loved His Father for all souls; for souls that love the Father and for souls that do not love Him. All our souls were in Jesus because He is the Head of regenerated humanity, the new Adam, in whom we are all spiritually present. All the holy love of souls, from the Virgin Mary to the last predestined, was present in Jesus, and He loves the Father for us all. What a consolation, what a joy that Jesus has loved and loves the Father for us, and that our poor love, before burning in our souls, has burned in Jesus' soul!

Alas! Many souls will not love the Father, but Jesus will love Him for them. The divine fire, which should have burned in them, will never burn, but this fire blazes in the divine Heart of Jesus. With what longing and intensity Jesus would love His Father for souls that would never love Him! With what eagerness would He not strive to ignite a spark of love for His Father, supplying for the deficiencies of souls with His great love!

The love of Jesus for His Father was a priestly love, that is, a love which glorifies, a love which immolates itself, a love which redeems and saves, a love crowned on Calvary and which is perpetuated in the Eucharist and in souls. It seems that Jesus wanted to fill earth, heaven, centuries and eternities with His love for the

Father. Just as the perfumed nard oil which anointed Jesus' head, spreading on His hair, filled the room with its fragrance, so also Jesus' love for His Father was poured out on Him, spreading over the whole Mystical Body and filling the world and history with His heavenly fragrance.

Our poor love is but the overflow of this divine anointing of Jesus which has extended even to our poor hearts.

Heavenly Father! Our love is very little and imperfect, very deficient and inconstant, but Jesus loved you for us, and this very meager love of our hearts passes through the Heart of your Son. Do You not perceive its fragrance? Do You not recognize the rich and unique fragrance of Jesus, as the scent of a flowery field blessed by the Lord?

In order to be Jesus, you must love the Father in the way Jesus loves Him. I say "in the way" not because your love can be ever equaled to the immense love of Jesus in intensity, perfection and richness that excel all forms of love, even that of the Virgin Mary; but I say "in this way" because your love must have the same fragrance as Jesus' love, being the faithful reproduction in miniature of Jesus' love.

You, too, must be all love, only love, always love for the Heavenly Father. All affections and actions of your life should merge into this divine passion. Especially your sufferings must have this ineffable love as their origin, center and life.

Your love for the Father must be unique, total, everlasting, ardent, tender, unselfish, active, like the love of Jesus; yours must be the love of self-abasement and adoration, of abandonment and sacrifice.

You, too, like Jesus, must love the Father on behalf of all your children and for all the souls that God has linked with you through the outstanding grace of spiritual maternity. In order to be a mother of souls, you must love on their behalf, as Jesus loved on behalf of all.

You must love for souls that love and for those that don't love. Many of your children love the Father, but the flame of love should first be in your heart before it can be in their hearts. Some of your children will love the Father with many limitations. You must supply for them. Perhaps some of them – may the Lord not permit it! – will never love. You must love for them. With what desire you must try to love for all in order that the Father may not lack even a spark of love from your spiritual family.

May the anointing which God also poured into your soul be like the divine nard expanding in all your children and filling the earth with its fragrance.

But above all, your love must be mystically priestly, that is, the love which glorifies, immolates itself, redeems and saves!

Your love, like that of Jesus, must find its crowning on the Cross, in Jesus' sacrifice, which is offered mystically in every moment, in your and your children's sacrifice, which is offered ceaselessly in union with Jesus.

You must suffer always because you must love always; you must suffer for all because you must love for all. Oh! May the sacrifice of love and suffering never cease in your soul: the offering of the Word, the offering of yourself, and the offering of your children.

You should be able to say to the Father: "Many of my children will not love You with perfection, but I want to love You perfectly for them. I beg You that there may be no one that will not love You, but if there should be some, I will love You for them. Since You have told me that I would have numerous descendants, so I love You on their behalf. Yes, I love You for all souls that will be associated with me until the end of time."

All your spiritual children should be able to say to the Heavenly Father: "My love is imperfect and small, but my mother loved You for me. Don't You recognize the fragrance of her love, which is the very fragrance of Jesus' love, in my heart's love?"

Your duty is immense, but do not be afraid, because in order to fulfill it you received and you will continue to receive in abundance the Gift of God, the Holy Spirit, the love which filled the divine Heart of Jesus.

Love with the Holy Spirit and your love will be like Jesus' love, as high as the sky, as deep as the ocean, pleasing to the Father and very fruitful for souls. So be it.[71]

November 24, 1928

SECOND DAY

Personal Reflection of Conchita

First Meditation

I simply continued to reflect on the Bishop's words, which contained so much.

Many times Jesus brought Morelia to my mind, and in the course of my prayer, it occurred to me to ask Him:

"But what do You want from this Archdiocese, my Jesus?"

"I want to pour Myself out," He answered, "to pour Myself out, above all, in My priests."

"And how?"

"Through your conduct in many ways; that is, by taking you and using you on their behalf and on behalf of their Shepherds."[72]

"But what good can I do for them?"

"You can give Me to them in many ways."

"Lord, You alone understand Yourself, because I don't understand You."

"It is enough for Me to understand Myself, even though you don't understand. You belong to the Church, and I will dispose of what is Mine as it pleases Me."[73]

"But what are You going to give to the Church in Morelia?"

"Above all, purity in many forms and in many ways. I want its clergy and its Shepherds to be distinguished by this virtue, this characteristic, this aspect. I will help them. I want this Church to shine with immaculate whiteness before My Father. Purity of souls, of bodies and of intentions; purity in their virtues, in their charity, in their love, in their sacrifices; always purity, always purity. (Jesus seemed to rejoice in saying this.)

"The priest who isn't pure, even though he belongs to the

Archdiocese, will not belong to it; that is, I will not take him into My Heart as such. I have always wanted to give this orientation to this Church, but now that I have united you to her, I want this more explicitly. In order that the Holy Spirit may reign here and nurture love and devotion to the Divine Word who leads toward the Father, I need pure hearts, pure souls, pure minds, pure atmosphere, pure souls without the darkness of sin and of what is less pure."

"How can I give them purity?"

"Imploring it, and spreading it by means of the Divine Word who dwells within you."

"But, practically?"

"By prayer, sacrifice, and the occasions which My goodness will put on your path.[74]

"The heads must be pure so that the members will be pure. My Heart hungers and thirsts for purity not only here for this Church, which I honor by special predilection, but also for the entire world. Because only by means of purity can My Father be seen and can souls come closer to God, in order to know Him and love Him. For this reason the Works of the Cross are My repose, since the seal of purity is their hallmark. And shall I say it to you? A reward for this beloved Archdiocese which has contributed so much to the Works is this: I want to refine its orientation in purity, purity, purity; and I am also going to tell you that for this reason I have brought you closer to it.

"To communicate purity, all its priests must be pure. And I solemnly promise you to reinforce the efforts of those of good will."

Oh, how good Jesus is!

The second and third reflection was on Bishop Martínez' same meditation.

My soul was moved to fervor and self-giving to Jesus without reserve.

Oh, Lord! I don't want distances, nor obstacles between Your Heart and mine. Break them, Jesus; destroy them, my Jesus, so that I may know how to live and die transformed into You, with Your same sentiments and heartbeats.

Counsels

1. Outside of God's manifest will, live always by faith.
2. If Jesus comes to me, very good, but if not, live on faith, that is, live on love.
3. I must intensify my interior life by means of my gaze of living faith in the mystical incarnation.
4. I must trust in Jesus and in my spiritual director, who represents Him.
5. I must dwell in peace.
6. I must take things *seriously*.
7. This is a golden counsel: *Neither look at myself, nor admire myself.* That is, I should not look for myself in anything; rather, I should disappear. Nor should I be surprised by God's graces, because everything that is good and great comes from Him. I will not look at myself. I will not be surprised at what He does.
8. "My love is a serious thing," Jesus said to a holy woman.
9. He is pleased in loving Me. I should be happy that *God is pleased with me.*

Special Graces

Purity.[75]
Fruitfulness.[76]
The grace of the mystical incarnation.[77]
So many lights on the Blessed Trinity!
Desolations.[78]
That my soul wasn't wounded by so many things.
Father Felix for the Works.[79]
Spiritual directors.[80]

I must:

1. live, above all, an interior life established on the theological virtues: faith, *hope* and love.
2. enter fully into the mystical incarnation, founded on the intimate relations with the Holy Trinity, with each Divine Person.[81]

I don't know how to give thanks to God for His goodness.

The Bishop dedicates to me the time I need; I listen to his talks, his counsels, his opinions as coming from God Himself, full of light and anointing; he pours the Holy Spirit into my soul.

> Thank you, my God, and reward him with more love
> for You.
> God enlightens him so much for the sake of my poor
> and thirsty soul.

Meditation of Archbishop Martínez

(On the Will). Having, like Jesus, the passion to always fulfill the Father's will, in all and perfectly.

You know that Jesus' nourishment was that divine will which not only was the only norm of His life, but also His joy and recompense.

Coming into the world, He said: "Behold, I come to do Your will, O God."[82] The thirty-three years of His life were the faithful fulfillment of His Father's dispositions, a living poem to His loving will. His death and sacrifice were the full accomplishment of that will, since the central point of the Father's will was the unique oblation of Christ's body, according to the teaching of St. Paul.

Jesus fulfilled *all* of His Father's will, either on Mt. Tabor or on Calvary, whether it glorified Him or it immolated Him. With what loving patience He awaited the hour of the Father, even though His Heart was ablaze with the desire for sacrificing Himself, saving souls and consummating His mission! At times, the Father's will contradicted Jesus' human will, as in Gethsemane. His sweat of blood could barely express the intimate agony of His will and nonetheless, in the midst of this cruel struggle, as a cry of His *triumphant love* for the Heavenly Father, there sprang forth from Jesus' lips and soul these words: "not My will, but Yours be done."[83] I have read somewhere that, perhaps, the cup which Jesus did not want to drink, was the martyrdom of knowing that many souls would be condemned in spite of His Passion. Who could perceive how much Jesus loves souls and the grief of His tender Heart upon seeing them condemned? Who could perceive the heroism of His love for the Father by His acceptance of the disposition of the divine will?

Jesus *always* fulfilled the will of His Father. Never in one of His acts, nor even in one single moment of His life, did Jesus act according to His own will; never was He *the lord* of His acts and life, because His love chained Him lovingly and freely to the Father's will.

Not only did Jesus do what was pleasing to the Father, but He did it as the Father wanted it, with ineffable delicacy. Even in details, Jesus yielded to the way which pleased His Father.

Biblical interpreters acknowledge that all the temptations that the devil placed before Jesus tended to turn Him away from the Father's will. With what faithfulness and love He overcame these temptations!

I can imagine Jesus consulting the Father's will at every step; speaking in our language, guessing His will, and not only the core of it, but its mode and details.

Jesus did what the Father wanted Him to do. The Father's will was the supreme motive of all His actions. Jesus knew the wisdom and love of His Father's designs, but even if He had not known that, it would have been enough for Him to know that the Father wanted it, in order for Him to embrace them with all His strength.

The Father's will was His joy and martyrdom.

It was His joy. To love someone is to will his good. God has but two goods: the essential that is He Himself, and the accidental, or extrinsic, that is the fulfillment of His will.

Jesus was pleased with the essential good of His Father with beatific joy, and He was pleased with fulfilling His will with loving delight. In my opinion, Jesus did not long for another recompense for His holy efforts, other than that of pleasing His Father perfectly, that of doing His holy will always and in all things.

That will was His interior and exterior martyrdom, because in all that He suffered, He suffered not only because the Father wanted it, but because the Father's will was His intimate and sweet sacrificer.

That very fine adherence to the Father's will and the divine passion to fulfill it, was the basis of Jesus' state of victimhood and His sacrifice. In the Psalms and in St. Paul, the fulfillment of the Father's will realized by Jesus is in opposition to the sacrifices and victims of the Old Covenant.

A victim is someone surrendered to the Father's will out of pure love and without conditions or reserve. A priest is a divinely anointed man destined to fulfill all the Father's will by means of the sacrifice which is its center.

St. Paul teaches us that we were all made holy by this will of the Father accomplished by Jesus' sacrifice. He shows us, consequently, that the only way to salvation for souls is the Father's will lovingly accomplished by every kind of sacrifice.

1. In order to be Jesus, you need to accomplish and love the Father's will in this way. You need Jesus' divine passion.

   You truly must say, as Jesus did, "*I always do what is pleasing to Him.*"[84] *All*, because not even one of your actions, or your instances, is to be anything other than the faithful fulfillment of the will of the Father. You are not the owner of yourself; you emptied yourself like Jesus, offering yourself to the Father's will as the blessed handmaid of love.
2. Adore, then, accept and love all that the Father disposes for you: joy or sorrow, desolation or consolation, silence or

speech, activity or inactivity. You must always live at peace, always happy, since you must always do the will of the Father.

3. *Always*, without interruptions, deficiencies, alternatives, or restrictions as far as your human weakness allows. May your life, as that of Jesus, be a living poem to the will of the Heavenly Father.
4. Like Jesus, you must accomplish the Father's will, surrendering with docility to the mode determined by Him, and accomplishing with loving faithfulness every detail He indicates to you. Like Jesus, raise your eyes to the Father to intuit His thoughts and discover His will. Oh, how necessary it is that your life be the faithful echo of the Father's will!
5. Do everything that the Father wants because He wants it; not just because it is your duty as His creature; not just because His will is so wise, loving and profitable, but you should fulfill it faithfully, because He wants it, because it pleases Him.
6. Basically, our love has two fundamental acts: to be pleased with the essential good of God and to be pleased with the fulfilling of His will. Consequently, you should have two fundamental joys (since joy is the fulfillment of love): the essential joy of God, in which you already share imperfectly by grace and in which you will share fully and eternally in glory, and the loving joy that the will of God will be accomplished.
7. That will that is your joy will also be your martyrdom, not only for all you suffer in order to adhere to His will, but also because often the will of God must be your intimate sacrificer.
8. Not only should you accept, love and adore what concerns you directly in the Father's will, but you should accept, adore and love this will for that which refers to all your spiritual children until the end of time. Accept all their sufferings and sacrifices; and when you think that some of them could

be condemned, share in the intimate agony of Jesus within your soul and cry out to the Father like Jesus, saying: "*Father, if You are willing, take this cup away from Me; still, not My will, but Yours be done.*"[85]

9. This full and loving acceptance of the Father's will should place you in the state of victimhood, *exposed* and *disposed* to everything that the Father may want; and also in the state of mystical priesthood, offering yourself and all your children to that will, beginning with Jesus.
10. In order to glorify the Father as Jesus did, one must love and fulfill His will even to sacrifice, even to the Cross. In order to save souls, one must do exactly the same.
11. Every immolation, every sacrifice, every cross is the perfect fulfillment of the Father's will.
12. That will is a martyrdom and a joy, a Calvary and a heaven, because it contains all sorrows and produces every joy. On earth, true happiness consists in accomplishing the Father's will with heavenly joy; that will which tortures and immolates.
13. This joy of fulfilling the Father's will is the holy, ineffable and divine joy of the Cross. Since the Cross is the supreme fulfillment of the Father's will, it is the supreme martyrdom and joy.
14. The passion of fulfilling the Father's will nailed Jesus to the Cross. He placed in it forever the secret of suffering and the secret of the joy merged into priestly love of His divine Heart.
15. All priestly souls must have the same passion of Jesus. This passion should nail them to the Cross where they will find suffering and joy fused in love.

November 25, 1928

THIRD DAY

Personal Reflection of Conchita

At night, Jesus spoke to me while I was "on the roses,"[86] and He continued during my first meditation.

Jesus continued as something already begun.

"But don't think that you must sacrifice yourself for Morelia only in Morelia, that is, for its Church, but for as long as I wish."

"Lord, is this because I am directed by Bishop Martínez?"

"For many profound reasons, and I will tell you that the heart of the Shepherds[87] has been and basically will be only one heart. He is far away, but he has been present through his love and sacrifices. I have purified him in many crucibles because of My high designs for him and for the good of his beloved and precious soul."

"Oh my Jesus! 'I am the Lord's servant' and for my poor sufferings give the beautiful treasure of Your purity to this beloved Church. Isn't it true that here You want to rest among the lilies? Do You remember that on other occasions when I came here You have spoken to me about purity?"

"The fragrance of this virtue attracts My Father's gaze and love, and My mercy. But look, for some time now – (and why will it be? Can't you see that it is the result of the reflection of My Works of the Cross because of the collaboration of Morelia in them?) – for some time now, I repeat, I have chosen souls from this Church with special predilection, with the incomparable color of this virtue of which I am so fond.

"Not so long ago and at many other times, Satan wanted to corrupt priestly hearts by his attacks; but I drove him back, and I will do so always pouring this cleanness, this innocence of My most pure Heart into priestly hearts. I desire that this chaste legion of priests and this city be distinguished in heaven and on earth by the special and evident color of this beloved purity.

"Oh daughter! The *Confidences*[88] will bring purity to the world, because they will bring many virtues along with it and, above all, they will bring, along with purity, the Holy Spirit of light, the eternal Focus of purity who will pour out purity into priestly hearts.

"What does the world need today? The purity of the Father, of the Son, of the Holy Spirit and of Mary. It needs very pure priests, and this reaction of purity in all its splendor, strength and activity should begin with Mexico and by way of the transformation of all priests into Jesus.

"This state of things through which the Church is passing, has been at the same time, a punishment and a grace, a purification and a reward. It won't take long to be understood. And how should My mercies be repaid? With purity, so that priests may be light, cleanliness, purity and by means of their full transformation into Jesus, spokesmen of the Holy Spirit. And here where you are, this clerical or strong and great priestly movement should develop, because of My great mercy and plans of help, redemption and purification for My Church, not only the Church in Mexico, but the Church universal.

"My Heart burns with desire for its fulfillment, but I need, above all, pure bodies, souls, minds and wills; purity of will is principal."

"But how is purity in the will?"

"How? By its likeness with the divine will which is always pure, luminous and holy. Oh, if all My priests were what I desire, soon they would hasten the triumph of My Church and that of the Holy Spirit in hearts."

"Lord, I have this doubt: isn't this to a great extent my imagination, because when Archbishop Ibarra directed me, You used to tell me many things about Puebla, and now, with Bishop Martínez, about Morelia?"

"Don't be afraid. I am the Lord and I have My times, and remember that not even one leaf of a tree moves without My willing it. Don't be afraid to follow always the way I mark you if you are obedient to My inspirations, when approved by your spiritual director, as a docile instrument of My will."

Later on, Jesus did not return to talk.

The Bishop's excellent meditations continue and I am delighted, asking Jesus, through Mary, to correct myself.

Meditation of Archbishop Martínez

To Be Jesus for Souls

Many considerations are unnecessary in order to appreciate what Jesus is for souls. It is enough for you to recall the sweet memories of your life so that, full of gratitude and love, you may discover what Jesus has been for you in your intimate experience.

How He has loved you!

With what unspeakable kindness He has treated you!

With what patience He has put up with you!

With what solicitude He has cared for you!

With what tenderness He has led you not only by the hand, but has also carried you in His arms and in His Heart!

What heavenly treasure He has poured into your soul!

With what delicacy He has dealt with you!

How He has thought about you from the days of His mortal life, in Bethlehem, Nazareth, the Upper Room and above all, on the Cross!

With what tenderness He loved you from that time on, from eternity!

How much He suffered for you!

How much your soul cost Him!

All His sufferings, He felt them before you did… more than you did… and pouring them out of His Heart into yours, He lovingly sweetened them!

There is no one ray of light which reached your soul, no one spark of love which enkindled your heart, no one virtue, no one gift, no one grace with which He enriched your soul, that Jesus did not prepare for you with exquisite care, that He did not warm with the tenderness of His Heart, that He did not purchase with the blood of His body and soul.

And He still has not finished revealing His love to you, pouring into your soul torrents of His tenderness, the inexhaustible treasure of His graces; He will still give you more, much more on earth and in eternity. Only in heaven will you know what Jesus has been, what He is and what He will be for your soul.

1. So what He has been for you, in due proportion, *you must be for souls*. He told us: "*As I have loved you, so you also should love one another.*" You must love souls as Jesus has loved you.
2. The measure of the love of neighbor is great! This is the love Jesus had for us. Rightly, St. Thérèse of the Child Jesus observes that we would be unable to fulfill the precept of charity toward our neighbor if Jesus did not dwell in us and if He Himself did not love him in us.
3. But you should notice that – given that Jesus does not love all souls in the same way – so not all souls must love others with the same perfection.
4. When a soul is loved more by Jesus, it should love others more, because it should love as Jesus loved it. How should you love souls? What should you do for them?
5. St. Thomas teaches us that the precept of love for God is unlimited; no matter how much we love Him, we always have the sweet obligation to love Him more; so that he who loves God more – no matter how much more – still has the obligation of loving God more.
6. Something similar should be said about love for souls. We always should love them more and he who loves more should love them more, since the measure of our love for them is the love that Jesus has for us.
7. Reflect… meditate… penetrate. How should you love souls? What should you be for them?
8. Jesus loved your soul with the same love with which He

loves His Father, as His Father has loved Him. "*As My Father loved Me, so I love you.*" Can you imagine greater love? Thus you must love souls.

9. Jesus loved you in order to redeem you, to save you at the cost of love and sacrifice. Thus you must love souls.
10. Jesus loved you in order to purify you, to sanctify you, to enrich you with His divine gifts. Thus you must love souls.
11. Ah! Jesus wants to continue to love souls in you, to sacrifice Himself on their behalf in you, to enlighten them, to inflame them with love, to purify them, to sanctify them and to endow souls with beatitude in you. What a sublime mission! What holy obligations! What unspeakable bliss!
12. Jesus' love for souls is a priestly love, that is, a love in which the words of St. Paul are fulfilled: "…*Christ, who through the eternal Spirit, offered Himself unblemished to God.*"[89] Priestly love has a divine source: *the Holy Spirit*; a divine character: *purity*; a divine purpose: *the Cross*; a divine fruit: *the sanctification of souls*; a divine end: *the glory of God.*

    Your love for souls, then, should be a priestly love; it should be distinguished by that holy zeal which burned in the heart of St. Paul, who said that he carried his spiritual children in his own heart and that he would spend everything and would spend himself on behalf of souls.
13. For many, for innumerable souls, you should be what Jesus is for all: *mother.*[90]

    You should beget them in your heart, giving them Jesus, who is life, by means of the divine fruitfulness of the Holy Spirit.

    This spiritual fruitfulness needs: (1) Purity as its source; (2) Love as its essence; (3) Suffering as its activity. Its goal is Jesus, who is divine purity, holy love and fruitful suffering in souls.
14. You must give birth to souls in suffering, in an unending, loving suffering, since souls never cease to be born on earth. St. Paul wrote: "*My children, I am going through the pain of*

giving birth to you all over again, until Christ is formed in you."[91]

You, too, should not get tired of giving birth to your children, constantly suffering terrible birth pangs and the unspeakable joy of birth.

15. And then you must nurse them: Jesus is the milk of little souls and He is also the solid food and the generous liqueur of mature ones. Jesus becomes our milk, adapting Himself to our littleness, and becomes our bread and wine when we have grown.
16. You must feed souls with your milk, that is, with your own spiritual substance, which in a certain sense, is Jesus. Being a mother, it pertains to you to adapt the divine food of Jesus to the littleness of your children. "*I fed you with milk*," said St. Paul, "*and not solid food, for you were not yet able to take it*."[92]
17. After you have fed your children with that divine milk, you must continue to nourish them with more solid food, with the most inebriating wine, giving them always Jesus, the only food of souls, until you are able to give them Jesus Crucified, whose suffering Body is the most solid food, and whose divine Blood is the most fiery wine.
18. Intimate relations with souls – and especially spiritual motherhood – have only one base, only one bond: Jesus. To give and to receive Jesus is what links souls together.

    With what exquisite care you should protect your children!

    With what tenderness you should warm them!

    With what care you should clothe them!

Purity is their protection; love is the fire which warms them; virtues are their clothes.

Your children must find consolation, strength, nourishment, joy and hope in you. In a word, all that you find in Jesus.

How beautiful it is to be Jesus for souls! One must feel their sorrows, their joys, progress and limitations within one's heart. St. Paul said: "*If anyone weakens, I am weakened as well; and when anyone is made to fall, I burn in agony myself*."[93]

For the love of souls the heart is dilated, resembling Jesus' Heart: it is dilated in love and suffering, in activity, in struggle and in victory. Love has something of the infinite about it and our heart is not sufficient for itself when it loves. How much we should thank God for giving us the ingenious way of loving Him with the hearts of others, of suffering with the sorrows of others, of glorifying Him with what other souls glorify Him! Truly, our love for God would seem truncated and almost desperate, if it were not united with our love of neighbor! What yearning for spiritual children souls touched by the fire of God's love feel! What longing there is on the spiritual level for the blessing like Abraham's, of having countless descendants like the stars of heaven!

Souls will be your joy and martyrdom; they will be your cross, that is, your suffering and rest, your immolation and heaven, as they were for Jesus.

All Jesus' sorrows and joys were two loves: His Father and souls! And these two loves are but one love, since the glory of the Father is the good of souls. Don't desire sorrows or joys other than those of Jesus.

For Jesus each soul is "unique," and He loves it as if no other one existed in the universe, and in this way He cares for it, and gives Himself to it, and in this way He sacrifices Himself for it. You must do the same; each soul that Jesus has entrusted to you should be "unique" in your heart's love, in your offering on its behalf; as St. Paul, you should become "all for all." One cannot give a piece of one's heart to a child, to a soul, but the entire heart; not an instant of one's life, but his entire life; not a drop of blood, but all the blood of one's veins and of one's soul.

Love for souls should have the same characteristics, according to St. Paul, as charity has: "*Love is patient, love is kind. It is not jealous, it is not pompous, it is not inflated, it is not rude, it does not seek its own interests, it is not quick-tempered, it does not brood over injury, it does not rejoice over wrongdoing, but rejoices with the truth. It bears all things, believes all things, hopes all things, endures all things.*"[94]

In a special way, you should have Jesus' patience for souls, which never gets tired, the kindness which makes His love sweet; the gentleness which never hurts, which always cures, and which fills the soul with delight even when it punishes, even when it scolds, even when it immolates.

Your love for souls should be like the love of God who loves all with all His Heart, but who gives to each soul the graces which correspond to its needs, according to His wise and loving designs. You should love all equally, in the sense that you should love them all with all your heart; yet you should love each soul to the degree that corresponds to God's designs for it. This subject is endless; but no matter how much can be written on it, the treasure of love, sacrifice, and holy fruitfulness which is enclosed in this profound formula could never be explained.

Love souls as Jesus has loved you.

Be Jesus for souls.

Personal Reflection of Conchita

This meditation impressed me very much and I reflected on it repeatedly.

Jesus communicated Himself to me again. I had thought, or rather felt, that He was so removed! May He be blessed!

I had long conversations with my spiritual director which were very profound and profitable, very instructive and full of anointing. They were like homilies.

Thank you, my God!

November 26, 1928

FOURTH DAY

Meditation of Archbishop Martínez

II. TO BE JESUS CRUCIFIED

Each transformed soul should be Jesus, but no one can reproduce Him in His richest fullness; but all essential traits of Jesus appear in all souls; in each one, something special about Jesus is emphasized and dominates: one mystery, one virtue, one character; and precisely this singular way of reproducing Jesus constitutes the mission of each soul; it marks its journey and indicates the place which it occupies in the Mystical Body of Christ.
You were fortunate to receive the best part, because your Jesus is Jesus Crucified; that is, Jesus in one of His supreme mysteries, in His most sublime mission, in His most exquisite love.

Yet, Jesus Crucified is an infinite abyss of light, life, love, suffering, perfections and He doesn't fit perfectly in any soul. I want to say that even though He gives Himself entirely to souls and reproduces Himself in them, there are still many ways of imitating the divine model. Even though many souls would reproduce Him, no one can reproduce Him in His fullness, but each one reproduces Him in its own way.

How Should You Reproduce Jesus Crucified?

1. Jesus Crucified is a Teacher, His Cross is a pulpit,[95] the highest one which has been raised up on earth. Even though Jesus was always a Teacher with divine pedagogy, He always revealed His heavenly doctrine gradually; and in every mystery of His life, He communicated different nuances of His unique doctrine to souls. At the twilight of His life He gave us the last lesson, the loftiest one, the most profound one, which is the basis of His doctrine – and this lesson He gave us on Calvary, and it is the doctrine of the Cross.

Undoubtedly, the Apostle St. Paul referred to that lesson when he determined to know nothing except Jesus Christ, and Him Crucified. The Church has taught that saving doctrine for twenty centuries, and thousands of saints – living interpreters of the Gospel – have explained its different aspects; and they have come closer to the unfathomable depth of that saving doctrine.

In this new epoch of history, in which hell seems to concentrate all of its strength in dealing the Church a definitive blow; in this epoch in which all heresies and errors are united to destroy the doctrine of the Church, and a new paganism has organized all vices and concupiscence, justifying them, increasing them, making them appear splendid by all modern means, and even divinizing them in a certain sense – God wanted to send His Spirit as in a new Pentecost, so that He might present the doctrine of the Cross to souls. This doctrine is explained, reflected in depth, attractive, divinely effective, greatly transcendent so as to oppose that earthly doctrine with the divine one and to oppose the modern paganism with that life of suffering and love; so as to oppose the phalanxes of hell with the army of the Cross formed by pure, loving and self-sacrificing souls, who will achieve more splendid and transcendent victory in the eternal halo of the Cross than that of Constantine when the holy *labarum*[96] appeared in the heavens.

This inscription could be placed at the foot of the Cross of the Apostolate[97]: "*In hoc signo vinces.*"[98] Now God wants to reveal to the world in a more perfect way the strength and richness of this new *labarum*, or rather the unique and immortal *Labarum*. It will bring a new and more perfect victory to the Church than that of Constantine, because this victory will be more spiritual and deeper, because this victory will bring the real freedom of the children of God which Jesus came to bring us, whose origin is truth, purity, love and suffering.

The Works of the Cross are the new lesson that Jesus gives to souls, perhaps the last one, or rather the ever old and ever new lesson, the same one He gave us on Calvary, but now the Holy Spirit clarifies it by the abundance of His light, and fills the divine

Heart of Jesus with delight; this lesson will be disseminated in souls like a divine explosion, as the blessed seed which is miraculously multiplied due to the efficacious fruitfulness which emanates from the Father.

The Works of the Cross are an ever old and ever new doctrine which, like a heavenly blessing, Jesus brings out of His divine and inexhaustible treasure, where there are things new and old, according to the Gospel.

Then you must be Jesus Crucified, not only by reproducing His suffering and by renewing His ineffable priestly love, but also because God has chosen you to give the world *the last* lesson of Jesus, the holy, fruitful, transforming lesson of Calvary through your instrumentality.

Modern science has produced marvelous inventions to diffuse sound at great distance without losing a tone, an accent, or its intensity. God desired to give the Works of the Cross to the world so that they might be reproducers, amplifiers, diffusers of that silent, living, eloquent, efficacious lesson that He gave to the world on the sublime pulpit of the Cross centuries ago.

Certainly, it is not enough for you and for yours to receive light and words in order to convey them to the world; no, the lesson of Calvary is neither reproduced, nor commented on, nor diffused except as Jesus gave it, that is, by means of the bloodstained body, the soul immersed in an abyss of bitterness, the heart burning with love, pierced by thorns, opened by the lance and crowned with the mysterious Cross.

The lesson of the Cross is luminous, interesting and efficacious when we live it. Truly, it is necessary to be Jesus Crucified either to give this lesson or to comment on it and to diffuse it. This is what you and yours must be.[99]

2. Jesus Crucified is a fountain of life. From His open wounds, from His pierced side, from the immense suffering of His soul, from the holy efficacy of His Blood – true, eternal life flowed out.

When Jesus was lifted up from the earth, He drew everyone

to Himself. When His side was pierced, the pure, immaculate, holy, fruitful and immortal Church came from it, as Eve had mystically come from the side of Adam.

Jesus had accomplished marvelous deeds in His mortal life, but all of them should have received their fulfillment, perfection and life on Calvary. In His public life He preached, but the light to understand His doctrine sprang forth from the Cross. In Nazareth, He taught the mysteries of the interior life, and in Bethlehem, the secrets of detachment, but the key to understand those prodigies is in the Cross.

In His mortal life Jesus had all heavenly and earthly delights, but in spite of it, He hardly drew souls to Himself. But after His Sacrifice, Jesus appears transfigured before souls; and those ineffable delights which were unnoticed by those who looked at them with their mortal eyes, became so alive and irresistible for souls who did not see them, that they produced a conflagration on earth, which produced euphoria and passion in souls; and even enveloped in the darkness of faith, these delights still need to be veiled in order that men do not die of love.

Jesus' fruitfulness comes from the Cross and from this blessed Cross all holy fruitfulness comes.

He who wants to be fruitful on the supernatural level, he who wants to have spiritual children, needs to go to Calvary, and to nail himself to the Cross, becoming Jesus Crucified.

An acorn is necessary in order to produce a holm oak; a Jesus is needed in order to produce or reproduce Jesus mystically. Just as an acorn has to die in order to produce a holm oak, so also he who is mystically Jesus needs to become Jesus Crucified in order to reproduce Jesus in souls.

The Works of the Cross must be a seedbed of holy souls. For this, in order to establish these Works, God made a living Cross and He wants each plant which grows in this seedbed to become a living Cross, too.

To be a living Cross is to be Jesus Crucified.

Jesus Crucified is Jesus in the Supreme Act of His Priesthood

All the acts of Jesus' life have a priestly character, but the essential act of His Priesthood is sacrifice. Jesus perpetuated this sacrifice in two ways: in the Eucharist and in souls. Consequently, there are two mystical sacrifices: the mystical immolation of the real Body of Jesus at Mass, and the real immolation of His mystical Body in souls. To these two sacrifices, then, the official sacrifice, properly speaking, and the mystical one, correspond two priesthoods. They both share in the unique Priesthood of Jesus.

All priestly sacrifice requires a priest, a victim and an altar. As the Church teaches us, Jesus was each one of these three things in the sacrifice of the Cross. These three things are present in the Sacrifice of the Mass and in the intimate sacrifice in souls, because we cannot be priests, victims or altars, except through Jesus and in Jesus.

The Priest

The priesthood has only one principle: love; one essence: immolation; one purpose: the glory of God. For this reason, the Holy Spirit, who is the personal love of God, is the source of all priesthood. The Holy Spirit is communicated to us, priests, in ordination, making us priests by imprinting on our souls the priestly character which is a participation in the Priesthood of Jesus. And on priestly souls, that is, on those who share in the Priesthood of Jesus mystically, but without the priestly character, the Holy Spirit is also poured out, because without Him no one can share in the Priesthood of Jesus. Yet, if the Holy Spirit is the principle of the priesthood, its essence is an intimate union with Jesus, a transformation into Him. Basically, this is what the Holy Spirit does when He forms a priest; He unites the priest to the supreme and unique Priest in a special way and transforms him into Jesus; He makes him another Jesus Crucified.

By means of priestly ordination, we priests receive this fundamental union with Jesus, this transformation into Him, which does not depend on our virtue, nor on our correspondence, because God did not want the essential priesthood to depend on the ups and downs of our liberty. But from this emerges the fundamental obligation of a priest, which is to make this transformation into Jesus full and perfect through love and holiness, since we receive its seed and basis in ordination.

In the mystical priesthood, the Holy Spirit unites priestly souls and Jesus transforms them into Himself by means of love, light and suffering. The purpose of both priesthoods is the glory of the Father. The sacrifice of Jesus is the supreme glorification of the Father and this sacrifice is renewed mystically on the altar and in souls.

A priest, then, is a man anointed by the Holy Spirit and united to Jesus by Him, so that the sacrifice of Jesus may be renewed for the glory of the Father and for the good of souls. The fruits of the sacrifice are always for the good of souls, and this good is the glorification of the Father.

A priestly soul is a soul possessed by the Holy Spirit and anointed by Him, so that He may unite it to Jesus through love and suffering; thus the soul can offer and immolate Jesus for the glory of the Father and on behalf of souls.

Basically, your mission consists in this mystical priesthood. The Works of the Cross are this mystical priesthood in which the souls who belong to them should participate in different forms and degrees.

In fact, all priestly sacrifice should have three parts: offering, immolation and communion. And Jesus is offered, immolated and received in communion in every sacrifice. You and yours must offer the Word to the Father; this is the oblation, the perpetual offertory of your unending Mass. This offering can have a formula, but this is not a formula. This is something very intimate; this is a whole interior life.

Personal Reflection of Conchita

The Chalice

Today Jesus spoke to me very early, before my meditation.

While I was "on the roses," there came the continuous pangs of interior sorrow like an agony. Once, not so long ago, Jesus explained to me that that state was a participation in His agony caused by the sins of priests.

"Look," He spoke to me when I was "on the roses," and later, "this immolation of body and soul purchases graces. Suffering is the coin by which graces are obtained."

"Then, Lord, how is it that this soul[100] purchases graces with love?"

"Because I had already purchased them with suffering; besides, love is sacrifice, immolation and offering; and then I unite My suffering (which embraces worlds and eternities) to the love which purchases graces.

"And look, the suffering which purchases graces carries love within; suffering alone would not be enough. When you offer Me your suffering, this suffering is the fruit of love, and its value comes from what it has from Me, since I am love which is not outside of Me, but is Myself. Since I consist of love and suffering as God and Man, both elements are always joined in different forms: love and suffering because they are Jesus, because they complete Jesus, because they cannot be separated from Jesus.

"The interior sorrow which expands in your soul is only a drop from My chalice, only a drop. What would My Heart feel with that sea of suffering? My great grace for you is to make you share in My interior, invisible chalice, which made all My life bitter. Do you know which is the bitter liqueur of that painful chalice? The sins of My priests which make My life most bitter and which hurt, pierce and offend Me; they would even kill My loving Heart, if that were possible."

"Lord, but when You lived, priests did not even exist?"

"They have always existed in My Father's mind, in the Heart of the Son, in the infinite charity of the Holy Spirit. And now, can't you guess why I share this bitter, sorrowful and painful chalice of My Heart with you? Since you belong to priests, you must bear the sins, infidelities, and miseries of priests in order to atone for them. In My special predilection I have desired to unite you to Me in this way so that you can console Me in what hurts Me most and elevate and perfect My priests, whom I love most in the world."

"Lord, don't speak to me in front of Mr. Augustine[101] (we were at Mass and he was helping)."

"I will communicate Myself when it pleases Me, and you should always be attentive to Me. I told you that that priestly suffering, if occasioned by the sins of priests and on their behalf, is one of the supreme degrees of charity; that is, to offer on behalf of priests the very suffering they cause. I did this and I continue to do it. For this reason punishments are stopped, for the loving immolation of the God-Man which the Father awaits because My charity – and that kind of sublime charity – impedes punishments, sweetens them or takes them away."

"Lord, I also offer the suffering of this sort of agony on behalf of priests."

"Because I have inspired you. All the good you do is not yours, but Mine. In your life, many of your actions and movements are not yours. It is not you, but I who orient and direct them."

Later

"Lord, what can I do to be more pure? This desire has grown in my soul and expanded its capacity."

"*Love Me* and *give purity*, because purity grows to the extent of love, and he who gives, receives."

"Listen, my Jesus, isn't it true that my soul grew in purity?"

"In purity and in light, because light is the radiation of infinite Purity, and purity is a derivation of Light itself."

"I am so pleased that that soul made progress. And You?"

"Can't you see that I am the author of all good? And in the soul who is disposed, I accomplish marvelous mercies and I pour Myself out.[102] I have already told you that I have My very vast purposes for that soul."[103]

"Dear Jesus, Morelia. Those priests who are making their retreat; I ask You to sanctify them equally, that You make them pure; don't tell me no; remember what You promised me last year? Isn't it true that You will make all of them, all priests of this place, very holy? Isn't it true that no one will be lost? I love them very much, and I will not leave this place without Your promise. Remember last night ("the roses," etc.)."

"What I promise is to distinguish them with special graces, giving them strength to take advantage of them."

"Remember Bishop Ruiz."[104]

"I have already told you that I love this soul very much; and I have desired to sanctify him in many crucibles."

"I want bishops to return,[105] and I want Your Church to be renewed and to flourish with holy priests."

"Much depends on this chosen part which I love so much. Its holiness will quicken it and ensure the triumph."

"Do You not desire to see Your glory, to be exalted in Your filled churches, and to be sacramentally exposed and triumphant?"

"And do you think that in these tragic moments I do not receive glory and very fine tributes in suffering? I certainly do, and I have My time. Remember that I told you that I am giving *a lesson of love*."

"Do You mind that I talk with You like this, without any order?"

"I'm pleased that you love Me, that you trust in Me, that you console Me, and that you purchase graces. I arrange things exactly in My good time, if souls respond."

"I don't want to leave this place."

"Wherever you are, I will be with you."

November 27 and 28, 1928

FIFTH AND SIXTH DAY

Personal Reflection of Conchita

Continuation of the previous meditation

Some days ago I felt something great, as if my soul had expanded. What did Jesus want? I was often reminded of what I experienced here in Morelia during my last retreat. When suddenly Jesus told me: "*I want to make you an echo of My love and of My suffering.*" And then the Confidences[106] came.

I felt that Jesus was willing to speak with me, so it came to my mind to ask Him:

"My Jesus, could You tell me what Your plan for Morelia is?"

"The plan of transforming priests, communities and souls into Me by means of the Holy Spirit and the Cross, and not only here, in this place, but in the whole Archdiocese."

"Lord, if You gave Your Heart… how can it be? You say that You are entirely in my soul by means of the mystical incarnation."

"It is true that mystically I am wholly in the soul, since I cannot separate My Divinity from My sacred humanity. But certainly I can make My presence felt when it pleases Me. The most delicate, intimate, loving and profound way is to make the soul feel the transfer of My Heart into the soul, since it is the center of My divine and human sentiments. This is the grace of delicate, loving and intimate predilection."

"What is the purpose, my Heaven?"

"That of divinizing the soul, of infusing into it, in greater or lesser degrees, My feelings, desires, inclinations and will. This is the most intimate manner of My entering ever more deeply into the soul, infusing in it what I am."

"Lord, why don't You give me this grace?"

"You already have it, My daughter, but you are unaware of My operations in your soul. It is called the grace of attraction, because I radiate in the soul. This is a very high point of transformation into Myself, which has its breadth and development in the mystical incarnation and which I grant to few souls to this extent."

"Lord, was this the grace of the exchange of Hearts which they say St. Catherine[107] had?"

"What do you want to know this for? I will tell you, however, that many of My saints went through the mystical incarnation without suspecting it, while the effect of this grace operated in them."

"Look, my Jesus, surrendered as You like to see me, I will ask a favor of You: that I may be aware of Your graces like that soul,[108] so that I will be able to thank You more."

"Let Me do as I wish; I prefer you to be blind, as I once told you."[109]

"So why do I desire this so much, even though it is not envy?"

"Because you don't surrender totally to My will. Many times graces are the same, because they have the same source, but I want that soul to be in light for himself and for others; and I want you to be in darkness for Me. Do you understand Me?"

"But in what darkness am I to be, Lord, with such a social life?"

"Even so, for My glory many will see in you My graces, of which you are unaware. Many of the graces which you have received have spread, but the core of My graces in your soul, even though you are unaware of them, are all for Me."

"Oh, I don't understand this mystery! You see that I am not allowed to delete from my *Account of Conscience* even my penances, which make me feel ashamed. This makes me feel embarrassed and brings me to tears."

"You can faintly see in your *Account of Conscience* these graces

I am speaking about, and they have been and are Mine. You don't understand, but your spiritual director does."

"Lord, I am an enigma to myself and I would like to see very clearly."

"But for Me, you are not. Let Me work in you without putting obstacles in the way."

"Does my spiritual director understand what only You see?"

"He understands what is sufficient, but in its totality only I, with My Father and the Holy Spirit, understand. Your soul, with all its graces, is the work of the Three."

"But is it not the same with all souls?"

"Essentially it is; the effects and special graces are not. I cultivate modesty and humility in souls with exquisite solicitude, and I know how to cover, as I covered your soul, with the veil of light, which makes the soul blind to its own splendors. I am always Light!"

"So why do You want me to be in darkness, which is contrary to You?"

"Because this darkness is the light of the Holy Spirit, which unites most, because it is Mine, all Mine, and not of the creature. This kind of light darkens and brightens; obscures, but at the same time shines for heaven.

"Many virtues, like faith and humility, are light and darkness. I am the way, so continue on it in peace, believing in the many works which I accomplish in you!"[110]

Meditation of Archbishop Martínez

Essentially, the interior life consists in the relations of our soul with God. These relations in priestly souls, in you and yours, should be priestly, as I explained above. You should allow the Holy Spirit to possess and anoint you, and, under His divine impulse, you should unite yourself to Jesus, offering Him to the Heavenly Father and offering yourself for His glory and the good of souls.

It is not enough to offer Jesus; He must be immolated. In Holy Mass, the consecration and the immolation are simultaneous. In the mystical Mass, you must become Jesus, be transformed into Him in order to immolate Him. Jesus, who is immolated by souls, dwells in those who have been transformed into Him. In order to immolate Jesus, souls must immolate themselves, because they are Jesus.

Don't think that it is boldness to say that we are Jesus. Isn't the Church the Mystical Body of Jesus, Jesus Himself, perpetuating Himself in the world? Are we not incorporated into Him? Are we not His members? Just as the whole soul is in each member of the body, so the whole Jesus is in each member of the Mystical Body. We are members of the body of the Church, and each one is destined to be Jesus. "*Admire and rejoice*," St. Augustine said, "*we have become Christ*." To immolate Jesus, then, is to immolate ourselves, but transformed into Jesus.

To the extent of our becoming Jesus, our sacrifice will be perfect. Our suffering and immolations are worth nothing in themselves, but if Jesus dwells and immolates Himself in us, He makes our smallest sacrifices precious and in a certain sense divine.

The perfect way of becoming Jesus is the transforming union, and the perfect way of becoming Jesus Crucified is the mystical incarnation. Jesus offered Himself through the Holy Spirit; He offered Himself unblemished to God, and He offered Himself to the Heavenly Father in the midst of great suffering. Priestly souls should offer and immolate themselves with immense love; they should offer themselves through the Holy Spirit. They should be unblemished like Jesus, and they should suffer with Him and in Him for the glory of the Father.

The perfection of the sacrifice depends on the degree of love, on the degree of purity, and on the perfection of suffering; it depends on the degree of the possession of the Holy Spirit, on union with Jesus, on the virtue that glorifies the Father in order that He may have His immolation.

Each sacrifice is consummated by communion, and in each communion we receive Jesus, and share in the Victim.

The first and supreme Communion is that of the Father, for this the Sacrifice is consummated in His bosom. The Communion of the Father is the acceptance of the Sacrifice, for which we pray at Mass through the words: "*suplices te rogamus*," etc. By means of the Holy Spirit, the holy Victim is taken to the sublime altar of heaven before the presence of the divine majesty, and the fruits of the Sacrifice descend on the Church and on souls. Our communion is the consequence of that divine Communion. The Communion of the Father is a communion of glory, and an abundant outpouring of goodness and mercy for souls is a consequence of that glory.

The mystery of the Trinity is an ineffable, essential and eternal communion which is realized in the bosom of God. But through sacrifice, in a certain sense, souls come to share in this divine communion. I think that this mystery is reflected in the doxology of the Canon: "*Per ipsum, et cum ipso, et in ipso est tibi Deo Patri omnipotenti, in unitate Spiritus Sancti, omnis honor et gloria per omnia saecula saeculorum.*"[111] These words are wonderfully linked with the part of the Canon which refers to the communion of the faithful.

Also in the mystical sacrifice, before any other communion, there is the Communion of the Father, the communion of glory. In the mystical sacrifice, too, the Holy Spirit leads the victim into the Father's presence, and from there the abundant fruits of the Sacrifice descend on souls.

The first one who receives Jesus in communion, after the Father, is the priest, and this Communion is necessary in the Sacrifice. Unfortunately, there is not always a fruitful communion of the priest in the Eucharistic Sacrifice; in the mystical one there always is. The Sacrifice supposes a transformation of the priest into Jesus, and by means of Communion, it realizes a new and perfect transformation into Him. Each Eucharistic Sacrifice should make the priest more perfectly Jesus. Each mystical sacrifice makes the soul who offers it more perfectly Jesus.

The faithful receive communion after the priest, and Jesus is diffused in souls like divine dew, like heavenly rain, like the holy radiation of light and love.

Souls, too, receive Jesus participating in the mystical sacrifice. For this reason priestly souls are fruitful; for this they have the secret of diffusing Jesus around themselves. Transformed into Jesus, they offer themselves with Jesus, and giving themselves, they give Jesus.

Sublime mission! The perfect realization of the longings of our soul! We thirst to give ourselves, because we thirst to love; but what do we give when we give ourselves, if we are misery and nothingness? Yet through this divine transformation, through this mysterious sacrifice, we give Jesus, giving ourselves; we pour Him out when we pour ourselves out. Thus we fulfill the desires of our hearts, the most ardent desires of the Heart of Jesus, and the desires of souls.

The Victim

Jesus is the only Victim pleasing to the Father. Yet through Him, in Him and with Him, we can and should offer and immolate ourselves. For this reason the priest has the obligation to be a victim and unite himself to Jesus in the Eucharistic Sacrifice, but not all of us accomplish this sacred duty. In the mystical sacrifice the priest is always the victim; if he were not a victim he would not be a priest, because he offers Jesus who dwells in him, Jesus into whom he has been transformed. We would say he is a priest because he is a victim, inasmuch as he who has received priestly ordination is a priest because of it, but he must complete his sacrifice in a certain sense through his free and loving immolation. Since Jesus is Priest, Victim and Altar, all who share in His Priesthood must share in the other two aspects.

We can clearly see the traits of a victim: it must be pure, intimately united to the great Victim and it must share in the priestly suffering of Jesus.

The Father is not simply pleased with suffering in itself, but with suffering in love and purity. A victim must be pure in itself, in its love and in its suffering. The purity of the victim is measured by its union with Jesus: Purity clothed with our flesh.

The purity of love consists in the lack of selfishness and in the adherence to the divine will. The victim does not choose its immolation, but it abandons and offers itself to the will of the sacrificer. Upon abandoning itself to this sovereign will, it embraces all forms of martyrdom through its disposition and desire. In its immolation the victim should seek or desire nothing but the glory of God, the manifestation of His attributes and the fulfillment of His will.

The purity of suffering should be measured by its origin, by itself and by its goal. By its origin, suffering is purer when it is holier and generous in its intention. The real and unique origin of pure suffering is the Holy Spirit, since this Divine Spirit can elevate the motive for suffering in souls more and more.

Priestly suffering is very pure, because it has very generous and selfless love as its origin. A priest does not suffer for himself; he does not immolate himself for himself, but for the glory of God and the good of souls. Undoubtedly, the soul who is both priest and victim can elevate all the suffering he endures as priestly, no matter what its cause. But sufferings which are priestly in the strict sense are those whose cause is the glory of God and the good of souls.

The purest priestly sufferings are those which – like Jesus' intimate sufferings – are suffered not only for the glory of God and the good of souls, but also when these most holy motives are their cause; that is, if the reason for this suffering is seeing the glory of God set aside along with evils and dangers for souls.

What purity and generosity these priestly sufferings have when they are caused by the very offenses of those for whom they are offered! Those of the divine Heart were like this; our sins were its origin. That Heart was crushed by them; they were His executioner. I think that the Heart of Jesus received the abyss of our sins, and when this abyss of malice met the abyss of love contained in that Heart, it was transformed into an abyss of suffering which made those who had caused it pure, holy and happy.

The purity of love in the heart of a priest and victim becomes the means by which suffering is transformed and thus purifies, redeems and transforms those who caused it by their malice. Can there be any greater likeness with the Heart of Jesus?

Suffering itself is purer when it is less mingled with consolation. Jesus' suffering was very pure, because it was a desolate suffering; in His supreme suffering He wanted to know even the mysterious abandonment by the Heavenly Father. For this reason the intimate suffering of souls who feel themselves abandoned by heaven and earth is particularly pure and fruitful.

The more divine the purpose of an immolation is, the purer it is. It is good and holy to suffer in order to atone for our own sins, but it is better and holier to atone for the sins of the others. It is good and holy to obtain graces for ourselves; but it is better and holier to obtain them for others.

To suffer for souls unknown to us, for enemies, to suffer without having the joy of even applying the fruit of our sufferings, but leaving all in God's hands, to suffer according to the most holy purposes of His will and according to His designs, to suffer identifying our own will with the holy divine will – this is to suffer with divine purity.

The mystical priesthood is destined to help the ministerial priesthood in many ways: acquiring vocations, cooperating in the sanctification of priests, making up for their deficiencies, atoning for their sins, converting and transforming them.

For this reason, the souls of the Cross must not only be priestly victims because of their identification with priestly immolation, but also because they offer themselves very specially on behalf of the official priesthood; they offer themselves for priests.

The immolation of the victims of the Cross should be priestly in its origin, that is, because its purpose is priestly; because this immolation has priestly characteristics in itself, and because its purpose is precisely to help the official priesthood in a hidden, but efficacious way.

What purity and priestly character must this immolation have![112]

The Altar[113]

The altar is a place where the victim is immolated, and from whence the fruits of the sacrifice are poured out because the blood of the victim is poured out. Undoubtedly, an altar should be pure, not only because of its lacking all stain, but also because of its need to be anointed by the Holy Spirit, the fount of purity.

Before Jesus' sacrifice nothing was pure on earth, since all purity, even that of the Virgin Mary, comes from that sacrifice. Before the Cross, the world was a quagmire on which the Father could not fix His holy gaze, nor could the Holy Spirit alight, just as the dove sent by Noah could not find a place on which to land on the earth inundated by the waters of the flood. Jesus was the first purity, and the only purity in itself which appeared on earth. For this reason He had to be the Altar of His sacrifice.

By His sacrifice Jesus purified souls, and He anointed them with His Spirit so that they might be altars on which His sacrifice could be perpetuated. The material altars purified by the Church are figures of Jesus, and symbols of the souls who are altars because they are Jesus.

No altar was as pure and holy as Mary; Jesus immolated Himself mystically in her heart; she was the purest altar, because she was Immaculate, and the holiest, because she received the fullness of the Holy Spirit.

A soul has to be very pure and filled with the Holy Spirit, in order to be the altar on which Jesus can be immolated. An altar is like an oasis in the desert, on which the Father can fix His gaze, and on which the Holy Spirit can alight; in a word, an altar is Jesus.

One can understand the intimate relations which exist among these three elements, priest, victim and altar, since they are different ways of participating in the states of Jesus, which are intimately united. We priests must be victims through our loving sacrifice and altars through our purity. The soul who shares in the mystical priesthood of Jesus must necessarily be priest, victim and altar, that is, it must be Jesus Crucified.

On the altar, the precious blood of the victim is poured out and the fruit of the sacrifice with it. From the altar rivers of graces, which emanate from the sacrifice, spring forth and flow everywhere. An altar is, then, an inexhaustible fount of divine graces.

Consequences

The immolation of Jesus is the essential act of the priesthood and from this essential act emerges the fatherhood of souls. St. Thomas teaches that the power which the priest has in the Mystical Body of Jesus, that is, his power over souls, is a consequence of the power he has on the real body, in the Eucharist. The priest is a father of souls, because, in a certain sense, he is a father of Jesus. He is a sanctifier of souls, because he is a sanctifier of Jesus.

The mystical priesthood has the same consequence. The priestly soul must be a mother of souls. Spiritual maternity on behalf of souls is but a natural extension on the supernatural level, that is, a logical extension of the relations of that soul with Jesus. Jesus is wonderfully diffusive, if I may be allowed to use this word. Being Jesus' mother, Mary had to be a mother of all souls, because Jesus is ineffably diffused in all. Since the priest has power over Jesus in the Eucharist, he has power over souls in which Jesus is diffused. The soul in which Jesus has been begotten, must generate Him in other souls, in which Jesus diffuses Himself according to His loving and wise designs.

For this, the mystical incarnation is marvelously fruitful; the soul cannot possess this grace without being diffused around, diffusing Jesus. One cannot be a mother of Jesus without being a mother of souls.[114]

The mystical incarnation is, therefore, the key to your spiritual life and mission; due to this outstanding grace you are mystically a priest, victim and altar; due to this grace, you are a mother of many souls; in a word, due to this grace you are Jesus Crucified, because these two words encompass what was said above, what we could say and what only God can say.[115]

The extension of this spiritual maternity, which derives from the grace of the mystical incarnation, is established by God according to His loving designs, which mark the measure of the grace granted to each soul, the mission of this soul, and the range of its radiation.

Our Lord indicates to you the extension of your maternity. It embraces all souls who belong to the Works of the Cross in one way or another.[116] And now He has revealed to you that it also embraces priests, because of the eminently priestly character of your mission.

With what amazing order God was preparing this new aspect of your mission! For many years, He has made you pray and offer sacrifices for priests. He established as the goal of the Works of the Cross to help priests in many ways. It seemed natural that, if the Works of the Cross lived the mystical priesthood, they should take on the mission of helping the official priesthood.

Last year, the Lord wanted to use you to show His plan for the sanctification for priests. He wanted to tell us what He suffered for us and what He waits for and desires from us.

The *Confidences*[117] is the doctrine of the Cross applied to priests. They are the commentary on the lesson given to us by Jesus from the Cross and received by St. John.

Yet, in fact, it is never enough simply to listen to the lesson, but it must be put into practice. The lesson of the Cross is so profound, so sublime, so difficult that, even though we know it perfectly, we are not able to put it into practice if the Lord does not send us His Spirit, as He did at Pentecost in order to apply the lesson of Calvary.

Jesus wants you to apply yourself to accomplishing what He desires to teach through you. Last year, He made you a speaker of His word. Now, He is making you a conduit of His efficacious and sanctifying action on behalf of His priests.

Everything depends on your being Jesus Crucified. Last year, Jesus Crucified was giving the lesson of the Cross to priests; now, Jesus Crucified must infuse in them the spirit of the Cross, which should convey to them the life of the Cross. Last year, you told priests that Jesus wanted them to be transformed into Himself by purity, love and suffering; now, Jesus wants you to help Him to put this transformation into practice.

November 28, 1928

SIXTH DAY

Personal Reflection of Conchita

Priests

Jesus said: "Do you know what the amplification you experience is? It is the generation of other souls, but especially the souls of priests. This is the most fruitful effect of the mystical incarnation. Since the Father begets the Word in souls by the Holy Spirit, that fruitfulness, due to its infinite origin, extends to souls; however, it has a priestly coloring and form in you, because it derives from Jesus, the High Priest. As I have told you, He was a Priest eternally in the understanding of the Father, and from this Priest all priests received life, being, fraternity and sonship with the Father.

"Because of this, in mystical incarnations it is natural for the Word to communicate to souls the priestly fruitfulness from the Father to a greater or lesser degree, since He is the first holy Fruit prepared by the Father and matured on the Cross so as to fuse all priests in Him.

"Consequently, this Work of the Cross must be priestly, because it is linked with the Incarnation of the Word and in virtue of it, with the mystical incarnation in your soul.

"What I am saying to you is very profound. All fruitfulness comes from the Father, but this priestly fruitfulness sown in the Word by the Father did not remain in the Word alone, since the Word communicates it to souls to the extent that it pleases Him, but total fruitfulness is only accomplished in mystical incarnations. It does not mean that the Word begets priests in souls, but that He communicates to them the fruitfulness which He received from the Father, who is the only one who begets His Son, the only one who, with His Son, begets other souls by the Holy Spirit.

"The Father is the only one who begets, but the Holy Spirit, by virtue of this divine fruitfulness, begets the Word in souls and makes priestly souls and the souls of priests fruitful with the Word, through the Word and in the Word.

"Motherhood of the Word does not exist for itself; it must extend to souls and its most striking aspect, its special color in Jesus, is the one in which the Father is most pleased, and which I communicate to certain souls out of the generosity of His charity; but only in its fullness, as was said, (taking into consideration the weakness of the creature) to chosen souls who have received the incomparable grace of the mystical incarnation.

"Can you see and understand what happens in your soul? Expand your soul, daughter, so that those priests who have divine brotherhood with the Word and to whom you must be a mother, may grow in it; receive the gift of God. All fruitfulness has its price and, if it gives life, it also takes it away, so to speak, in the sense of sacrifice. Yet is this of any importance, if God is glorified by it?

"You belong to the Church in a very special manner; can there be any greater honor and blessedness for you than that of giving it holy priests?"[118]

"Lord, I know that they are babies when they are generated; when will these priests give You glory, especially in a spiritual sense?"

"Do not confuse the material with the spiritual in your understanding. You generate souls and not bodies, and souls don't have size, because they are divine. They are the image of the Trinity that is measureless, that fills everything, and all exists eternally in its infinite bosom. This is a mystical kind of generation, spiritual and holy, and its goal is to purchase graces for those who are generated.

"And because I want this priestly aspect of your Jesus to be distinguished in you, for this you have to enlarge the recesses of your soul, so that thousands and thousands of souls may fit into it; not in the material capacity, since souls don't have measure, as I have told you, but in the capacity of purity, sacrifice and exterior or interior activity, which is most fruitful, according to what I want to give you.

"In this retreat, I want you to accept freely this gift of begetting holy priests, which the Father granted to you when He begot the Word in you. I want you to give them life with your life, blood and purity. I want you to give them virtues and holiness by means of your sacrifices united to those of the Word which give them merit and supernatural value for heaven. Understand that this is not a mere formula, but the divine extension of the mystical incarnation in your soul for the honor of the Trinity and good of priestly souls."[119]

"Lord, You told me once that I should be the mother of priests."

"Yes, I already announced it to you, but now I want this fruitfulness – which derives from the Word and proceeds from the Father – to start working in your soul. I want you, purified and content, to accept it in all its parts and with all its consequences. May your spiritual director choose the day to offer you to the Trinity for this purpose, and may you, humiliated and lovingly trustful, accept without conditions these new sons in the Son, these priests in the High Priest. Now the mystical incarnation of priests is to be realized in your soul by means of Mary; through the Word and in union with the Word, you will have the agreeable task of offering them to the Father. Certainly, if this act is accomplished here, priests from Morelia will be first of the great number of priests to occupy your heart."

"Will they and You all fit into it?"

"Thousands of heavens and all souls would fit into Me and I into you, by virtue of My unity."

Later on, Jesus told me:

"As you accept this maternity, which derives from the mystical incarnation, you must suffer in union with Me for the sins of priests, which wound My Heart so much. You must drink from this chalice, which is very bitter to My soul. You must experience the suffering of My interior passion, which was the most painful and cruel, but at the same time was the greatest source of purification for others and of imploring graces for them.

"Yet remember and be consoled by this thought: *that of knowing that you console Me.* You must activate your interior life so as to implore heavenly graces in order to make these priestly hearts fruitful. You must atone in yourself for those sins which torture your Jesus: those of the altar and those of the ministers which I have intentionally specified to you in the *Confidences.*

"You must be a mother, with all a mother's sacrifices, offering Me in your heart for the guilty and also offering Me so as to snatch graces and gifts to sanctify those of good will."

"Lord, will the bishops enter in all this?"

"Are they not priests?"

I had many struggles and Satan tried to inflate that immense burden which I was willingly taking on. Above all, I was scared, terrified, so afraid that I fought against it and I couldn't; so I ran full of struggle, fear and fright to the room where my spiritual director was, because I didn't want to accept God's will. I talked with him to get it off my chest, and he supported me, convinced and strengthened me.

He told me that at the beginning of this retreat he struggled with Satan and he was unable to write anything. But all that was a good sign.

Later on, Jesus told me:

"Go on, daughter; may nothing hinder your running the race of Calvary. May the divine love be your guide and generosity your compass.

"As I have already told you, Mary begot Jesus along with the fruitful fiber of the priesthood. At the foot of the Cross, in the person of St. John, she received all as her children, especially priests."

"Lord, where will those from the Oases stay, whom You say are my spiritual children?"

"In their place; but this new tinge of receiving priests as sons of your soul is only the amplification, even though in the highest degree, because it is united more perfectly with the Divine Word.

"All Works of the Cross are priestly, because they have received this radiation and this orientation through the Word. This amplification of your soul will crown the Works, giving them splendor once this plan is accomplished. These Works receive this priestly charism from heaven in you, in union with the Word. This charism will glorify the Father and it will only be the extension of that Divine Word in what He loves most, in what belongs to Him, in what is most delicate, in His other sons, who are also Jesus."

November 29, 1928

SEVENTH DAY

Meditation of Bishop Martínez

How is Jesus and He Crucified?

You already know that only the Holy Spirit and Mary can form Jesus and, consequently, you should have intimate relations with them. Do you know which ones? Keeping the right proportion, the same ones which Jesus had with them.

These craftsmen form Jesus perfectly by means of the transforming union, and Jesus Crucified by the mystical incarnation. So you began to be Jesus Crucified by this outstanding grace and from the moment you received it you did not have other obligations than those of developing its consequences fully and perfectly.

The consequences of this grace are the doctrine of the Cross, the Works and charisms with which God has enriched your soul. That doctrine, those graces and those Works have the same purpose as the sacrifice of Jesus, that is, they are eminently priestly. They all carry the characteristics of Jesus Crucified, that is, purity, love and suffering.

All that you have received has a priestly aspect because its center is the mystical incarnation, not only in the sense that all this constitutes or surrounds the mystical priesthood, which is the heart of your mission, but also because all is directed to the efficacy of the official priesthood.

In reality, God has charged you to care for priests and you have always worked for them, since the priesthood is the purpose of your doctrine and Works.

Our Lord, who always puts the seal of order and unity on His Works, wants you – after you have contributed to this very high goal by the means which He has inspired you to use – to ascend higher and touch this end even more directly; that is, that you not only work in order to form souls who must pray and sacrifice themselves for priests, but also that your soul may arrive at the ultimate consequences of the mystical incarnation and thus give yourself fully and directly to achieve the purpose of your Works and mission.

As a general in charge who disposes all for combat, dispatches the army and directs the fight, when he reaches the last battle, goes personally to make the last attack, to take the last position and to plant his standard on the conquered territory; so Jesus in you, *after having said* and *done* many things for the sanctification of His priests, having given the plan of combat in your writings and forming the army of your sons and daughters of the Cross, now He Himself wants to direct Himself personally through you to priests. First, He tells them what He wants from them by means of the *Confidences*; now He asks you to offer yourself fully and totally on their behalf. To be Jesus Crucified you had to have done many things in different periods of your life, or rather, God in you. To be Jesus Crucified you had to have practiced many virtues, to have assimilated His intimate sentiments in your heart, to have suffered His internal and external sorrows in order to accomplish His Work. Now, to be Jesus Crucified is to *offer yourself totally*, *fully* and *lovingly on behalf of priests and the Church*, as Our Lord has asked you. This is the crowning of your life and your Works.

This way of being Jesus Crucified encompasses the purest, most exquisite, effective, extensive and fruitful *priestly love* of the Heart of Jesus. It encompasses His *most intimate suffering*, which is consequently very bitter and thus fruitful. It encompasses His purity *in the highest degree*, since there is nothing purer because there is nothing more divine than having the fullness of purity which overflows, purifying souls. It encompasses His divine fruitfulness, since as the Church and especially the priesthood sprang from His Heart, so also from the love and suffering of the Heart of Jesus that you carry in your heart, sanctifying graces will flow for the Church and especially for priests.

What a sublime mission! What glory you will give to the Father! What a consolation for Jesus! What a repose for the Holy Spirit! What a joy for Mary! What a life for the Church! What a divine stimulus for priests! What a transformation for souls!

In this new period of your life *all your duties*, your *unique* manner of being Jesus Crucified in the here and now, are to make your total offering on behalf of priests tomorrow as Jesus asked you to and to live it perfectly afterwards.

In order to live this offering, you need *to believe* without hesitation; *to trust* without measure; *to abandon* yourself without reserve; that is, you need to exercise the theological virtues in a perfect and heroic manner.

Above all, you need *to believe*, because in all stages of the Christian life, faith is fundamental. One only hopes for what one believes in. One only loves what one believes in. One only acts according to what one believes. One only lives what one believes.

Is what you must believe very high? It is not higher than the divine mysteries; and when God speaks, nothing is high, because God is infinite in all. All is amazing in what God says, because all surpasses our poor understanding; but nothing that is related to God is amazing. Is it amazing that God says and does very high things? It would be unusual if He did not.

But you could say that faith in the mysteries of God is guaranteed by the Church, which is Jesus Himself. In fact, faith in what God says and asks for is guaranteed, too, by obedience. For you, this guarantee is decisive.

Everything should be believed because everything has the same basis, that is, the word of God guaranteed by obedience; and you must believe *without hesitation*, because faith is very firm, and you must believe *blindly*, because faith is blind.

After believing, you must *trust*. Don't look at yourself, because you by yourself cannot lift even a straw from the floor. How many times distrust comes from that anxiety – apparently incurable – of looking at ourselves!

Don't look at yourself, because you are nothing; because you are nothing, you are worth nothing, and should not even take yourself *into consideration*. Look at Jesus; rely on His love, strength, wisdom and power. With this support, how can you not trust? St. Paul said: "*Omnia possum in eo qui me confortat*."[120] We can and should say this, because St. Paul said it, not because he was St. Paul, but because he relied on Jesus; and Jesus is always the same.

When St. Paul was looking at himself, he used to say: "*Nihil sum*," meaning "I am nothing." He also wrote that he would rather glory in his infirmities; but when he wasn't looking at himself, but rather at Jesus, he said that he felt capable of everything.

Don't look at yourself, and if you do, look at yourself as at the immense emptiness which God fills; look upon yourself as a "nothing which relies on God's power" and say with the Apostle: "*Cum enim infirmor tunc potens sum*."[121]

Don't limit your *confidence*, because the power, goodness and love of God have no limits. Hope, like Abraham, against all hope, that is, even though you feel that all the world and hell unite against you; even though you see around you darkness and desolation; even though it seems to you that God abandons you, *trust always*, *trust in spite of all*, *trust without measure*, because heaven and earth will pass away, but the love and fidelity of God will never be lacking.

Rest in the word of God, in Jesus' love, in His promises; cast yourself into the bosom of God with no solicitude, with no care, like a child in its mother's lap.

After telling you about confidence, I must tell you about *loving abandonment*, which is your primary duty. Love takes all forms, according to the stages of the spiritual life and God's designs. Your particular form of love should be total and perfect abandonment to the divine will, which is the highest and purest form of love. Basically, what is the "offering" you are going to do tomorrow, if not an act of loving and full abandonment to God's will for the sake of that great work to which you were destined?

Really, to have the same suffering and joy of Jesus, to share in His chalice and His interior cross, effectively means the fusion of wills, a very close union of hearts, which requires loving and full abandonment to the divine will. You will no longer have your own will, and consequently, no longer your own desires, pains and joys. Instead, Jesus will dwell in you fully, in the sovereignty of His love, with your being and life in the possession of His divine will.

You will penetrate insofar as possible into the intimate depths of the divine Heart, into the deep recesses of that Heart, according to God's designs; and you will feel the most exquisite fibers of that Heart vibrate in yours; and His most intimate palpitations will be yours. The same thorns will crown both hearts fused into one; the same lance will pierce them both; the same intimate cross will crown them.

Blessed are you who have been invited to penetrate into what is most precious, sweet, and exquisite in the divine Heart: into the depth of His priestly love and suffering.

Don't pull the chalice of the divine will away from your lips, nor the intimate bitterness of Jesus from your heart. You already know that if that chalice and bitterness make you share in the agony of Gethsemane, not an angel, but Jesus Himself will comfort and console you, as He has promised you since 1894.[122]

Your present path has become marvelously simplified, with a divine simplicity, that is, in accepting without reservations, conditions or limitations, but rather, in accepting the will of God perfectly, fully and lovingly.

I have already explained to you how that abandonment to the divine will does not extinguish nor diminish the thirst of loving and suffering, but rather how it exacerbates it in an incredible way, because the cross is the center of the will of the Father.

That full and loving abandonment will make your union with Jesus closer and more intimate, and it will accomplish the ineffable and supreme desire of Jesus, which He expressed to His Father in the Upper Room: "*So that they may all be one, as You,*

Father, are in Me and I in You, that they also may be one in us… I in them and You in Me, that they may be brought to perfection as one, that the world may know that You sent Me, and that You loved them even as You loved Me."[123]

Personal Reflection of Conchita

Jesus spoke about priests

I was filled with constant spiritual joy, and my soul was inundated with peace. When I was "on the roses" Jesus said to me:

"I did not want to tell you everything yesterday; but look, My daughter, the pope, cardinals, archbishops and bishops, parish priests and priests should enter into full acceptance of that spiritual motherhood on behalf of priests. So now you must immolate yourself for their sake, because the entire ecclesiastical hierarchy forms one priesthood with the Eternal Priest.

"But don't be frightened; this is only one way of manifesting My plans to you by emphasizing them; but when you received Me into your soul in the mystical incarnation, you received Me and in Me My Church with all its priests. I cannot be separated from this holy and heavenly fiber which constituted the reason for My coming into the world: My universal priesthood is nothing other than My infinite charity to save it. The Father found no better way to save the world, so to speak, than the priesthood which forms the body of the Church and whose center, or heart, is the Trinity itself. For this reason, the Word became flesh primarily in order to be a Priest and to extend this priesthood in chosen souls.

"Thus the spiritual and mystical priesthood derives from this. When you received the Word mystically incarnate in your soul, together with Him, the Eternal Priest, you received all priests. Since I have chosen you from eternity for the Works of the Cross, which are in their beginning, middle and end priestly works due to the Holy Spirit, you must distinguish yourself in this pure, holy, and fruitful immolation on behalf of the Church, that is, on behalf of its priests. Pray much for the pope, daughter; carry him in the depth of your soul, and carry with him the weight of the Church, with all who form it, without any exception.

"Now, I ask you to translate into action – with all your understanding and loving generosity – My longing that you receive into your heart, not only a nucleus of souls, but also the weight of the Church. I will help you. Without Me, you couldn't bear it, but with Me in you, why should you be afraid?

"Certainly, I have already used you in this way; but now I am asking you for a total, complete and everlasting offering for My Church so that all your works, sufferings and immolations may be for priests in all their grades.

"Even more, it is your duty, insofar as you are able, to lead priests to heaven. Also the souls of the priests who are in purgatory belong to you, so that you may hasten the beatific vision for them. But look, daughter, at My great mercy for you: in each saved priest, I will see something of yours which will glorify Me. You don't understand the extent of this divine promise, which will increase your glory, but your spiritual director does. So do not be afraid. With all the generosity you are capable of, cast yourself toward the only north of your life, which should be My will, glorifying the Trinity. Why should you be afraid, if I live in you and will be your strength?

"Expand your soul and enjoy the painful Cross which My goodness offers you, because to be a mother is to be a living Cross."

"Lord, so don't You want me for the Works of the Cross any more, as You have told me many times?"

"Yes, you will continue to be for the Works, but in a more perfect and profitable way. From now on, you belong to priests and all your immolations in union with Me will be for priests.

"Not only this, daughter, but you must also consecrate your life, not only for ordained priests, but also for those in formation, for seminarians, for hesitating vocations and for those whom the o snatch, because your mission extends to all of them, inning to the end, in those sublime priestly races.

"Don't you want to save the world? Didn't you ask Me this with your blood before the Works were founded? Why did the Works come into the world? If you really want to save souls, we have arrived at the powerful and unique means: *holy priests.* They will be holy to the extent that you become holy; they will be pure to the extent that you are pure; and they will become holy to the extent of your sacrifices. But all this not because of what you are, but because of what you have in you, because of your union with the Word by the mystical incarnation, because of My infinite merits which you have in your hands because you have Me in your heart.

"Oh yes, daughter, this is the crowning of the Works of the Cross, and your spiritual children will follow this plan to a lesser or greater extent; this will be the real consolation for My Heart: *to give Me holy priests.*

"By means of the *Confidences*, I have already made you know the difficulties which priests must overcome; consecrate yourself, so that they may avoid them."

"But how, Lord?"

"By purity, suffering, love and virtues practiced on their behalf; by the agonies of your soul, by the chalices which I will put to your lips and in your heart. Yet, don't be afraid, since what I will give you, will first pass through Me, who communicate power and strength to the crosses, helping you likewise to endure them.

"Tell Me that you do accept, that you do abandon yourself to My will, that in union with Me you will belong to priests forever, because your mission for their sake will continue even in heaven.[124]

"But consider another martyrdom, which encompasses all others: what priests do against Me, you will feel; their sins will make a martyr of you; their lukewarmness will make you ache; and their ingratitude could kill you. Because, basically, your being associated with My priesthood in them consists in this: that you may feel and suffer for their unfaithfulness and miseries in the measure in which I – the pure, holy and divine Priest from whom priestly grace comes – suffer for them.

"Meditate on these points conscientiously and offer yourself to My will, to My desires which I convey to you today, with all the fire of your soul and all your immense love.

"You will struggle; all hell will rise up against you; but why are you afraid, if you have Me, if you belong to the Eternal Priest, who wants to renew priestly fervor from the bottom up, and to transform priests into Me, guiding the Church thus to its real foundation and glorious goal?

"Tell that soul to be the first to welcome My desires with respect and love and to put them into practice."

Later on, Jesus said: "If it is an honor for a mother to give her son to the Church, won't it be the same for you if, in a certain sense, you accept and give spiritual life to so many children?

"In this way you give glory to the Trinity more than in any other way, and through the Word, Priest and Victim, you will attract the loving gazes of the Father toward this world and His Church, and the gifts of the Holy Spirit for those who serve it.

"It is right that you feel embarrassed by this grace, because it is an outstanding grace to unite you to Me in this form on behalf of *My priests*, whom I love most on earth; but it is right, too, that you should feel honored and thank Me for this distinction.

"Why do you think I granted this to you? Because of what you are to Me in the mystical incarnation; and to guide My brother priests by the purest bonds of brotherhood toward My Father, who is their Father."

"But, Lord, have You not always done so and in this way?"

"Yes, by means of Mary, the first priest,[125] who in giving birth to Me, gave birth to the priesthood – whose Head I was – in her most pure womb. And as a reflection of Mary because of the mystical incarnation, the same is true of you in the least degree, since this grace proceeds from the same grace and from the same source. I took into your soul's womb with Me the same priestly fiber which accompanied Me in Mary; it germinated in you with My grace and I nurtured it with loving solicitude. And today it has reached its development, as I seek from you the most holy fruit of this grace in My priests: your spiritual motherhood on their behalf, fully and freely accepted in the fullness of its purity and suffering."

Later on

I asked Jesus: "Lord, I resist giving them all, all to priests, because I have my children[126] at home and it is my duty to purchase graces for them."

"This same sacrifice will be on their behalf too, very much on their behalf, I promise it to you. Besides, I am taking care of them. Anyway, your giving yourself on behalf of priests and giving them all does not hinder you from imploring graces for your children, since that is a motherly duty."

"Lord, tell me, did You bring me to Morelia now for what refers to priests?"

"Can't you see? I prepared My plan in My silence and I wished to come here to consolidate it for My high purposes. Do you remember that I told you in this precise place that I wanted to make you an echo of My loves and sufferings?[127] I fulfilled that promise by *Confidences* and I wanted it to come to its fulfillment here too. Those priests, in their struggles and triumphs, in their sorrows and combats, will vibrate in your soul as they do in Mine, forming the same echo in My Heart and in yours.

"Another secret on your behalf is that from now on My union with your soul will be closer and more intimate, because I have led you to the summit of My greatest sufferings: priests, and to My greatest loves: priests.

"We will have the same causes of our suffering and the same effects in the sufferings of love. You will be more essentially Mine; you will be fused into My sentiments and under the gaze of the Trinity we will form only one Heart, only one soul glorifying this Trinity.

"You cannot understand – although your spiritual director does – how profound this grace is and what its consequences are. You are unable to measure its extension, but thank Me, even though you do not understand its range, and let your spiritual director thank Me for it."

"Lord, I ask You only one thing. May this grace be unnoticed by the world. Will You grant it to me?"

"Yes, in part, but I cannot promise this with regard to its effects. Don't you see that I want to be seen through you when it pleases Me? If we have the same sentiments, won't you arrive at the point of My transformation into you through My grace, which is the one you should communicate to My priests? You take care of Me in priests, and I will take care of you in them."

My God and what a burden! I feel annihilated.

November 30, 1928

EIGHTH DAY

Personal Reflection of Conchita

The feast of St. Andrew the Apostle

My director chose this day for my "Offering," which he wanted me to write personally.

During Mass, after the Consecration, I read it to my Jesus with all the generosity of my poor soul.

Before copying it here, I will write first what Jesus told me while I was "on the roses" and doing other penances, etc. Over a period of several days, I offered my Jesus nard sprinkled with my blood close to the veiled Tabernacle.

This is what Jesus told me when I was "on the roses":

"We will call this day the day of *Triumph*, because I will triumph over hell through you once more on behalf of My Church and the spiritual good of My priests. Look, today you will offer that flower to the one who now represents the Church here,[128] as a sign of the pact of your commitment with it; the pact of purity and blood which will yield excellent fruit for Me if priests correspond to My graces."

"Ah, Jesus! Don't leave it as a probability, because You can make them correspond."

"What I promise you is to appeal to their souls strongly by means of the Holy Spirit, so that they may be spiritualized by intense interior life, and be transformed into Me."

"Lord, grant to Archbishop Ruiz and to my spiritual director the fullness of transformation into You; besides, don't they say that bishops have the fullness of the Holy Spirit?"

"I promise you to guide their souls to that goal if they correspond."

"And if they don't, will You give it anyhow?"

"Well, for My part, I am faithful."

"So thank You, thank You, my Jesus. On this day of the Triumph You will grant me many graces. Are You pleased?"

"In triumphs the heart is always happy."

"So grant me to triumph over myself in all that could hurt You."

"Done."

(And I presented Him my petitions which, I am sure, He listened to with much love.)

"Lord," I told to Him, "I feel that I belong more to You, even as I offer myself on behalf of priests."

"Well, in them you give yourself to Me. I am very glad."

Today sixty-five seminarians who are studying theology are also concluding their retreat. May the Lord make them holy.

Immediately afterwards, I put down my *Prayer of Offering*.

Prayer of Offering

Jesus of my soul! In the presence of the Holy Trinity, and through the immaculate hands of Mary, I make the absolute, total and unconditional offering of myself on behalf of priests to You, embracing the entire spectrum of what Your loving will has ordained for me.

In union with You, I offer You my belonging to priests forever. I am embarrassed to say this, but I want to carry the Holy Father, with the entire burden of the beloved Church – cardinals, archbishops, bishops, parish priests, priests and finally seminarians – with their hesitations and vocational struggles – in my soul. I will also belong to deceased priests, offering suffrage on their behalf to lead them to heaven.

And all this, Lord, trying to be really *Jesus Crucified*. I accept with loving enthusiasm, with purity and suffering, with the virtues and agonies of my soul, drinking to the dregs all the chalices of suffering which Your will may send me; I adore Your will with fervent love and I clasp it closely to my heart, which is Yours.

Yes, my adorable Jesus, from now till my death, with the help of Your grace, I embrace Your holy will, which honors me without any merit on my part, and which crucifies me. But I want to go beyond, to the delicacy of love, to the exquisite perfection of love which You have taught me. I want to accept this entire world of priestly souls, hidden crucifixions, unnoted Calvaries and untold bitterness, *only for love*, happy to help You, only, only to console Your beloved Heart, only to please Your will, even though it may torture, crucify and kill me!

I want to help You with Your interior cross. I want to accompany You and share in Your intimate bitterness which makes You suffer so much. I want to be pure for those who are not; I want to sacrifice myself for those who do not; I want to thank You for the ungrateful ones, and to be a mother, a victim, and to give all the blood of my body and soul for the transformation of priests into You.

I am very weak, but You are my strength. I am nothing, but I have You who are all. For this I beg You, Jesus, with all the fervor my poor love is capable of, that You may use me in any form it pleases You for the good of the beloved Church and the whole hierarchy, which I love and respect with all my being. May this offering be the happy crowning of the Works of the Cross, and may the same sentiment and blessed immolation continue after my death until the end of time in those who belong to me.

I will be happy in serving You in what You love most. I will be happy if the Blessed Trinity would receive all the moments of my life from now till the last breath of my agony on behalf of those beloved priests. I will be Yours, I will be a mother, I will be a victim for their sake on earth. I will also turn my heaven into serving them for Your love. Amen.

After this offering, my soul was full of joy, and my spiritual director congratulated me when he read it.

Oh, Jesus, Jesus of my life! Is this all possible?

Oh, my Lord, may You be blessed!

Meditation of Archbishop Martínez

Counsels

The fruit of your retreat is your offering made today, and your resolution should be to live it perfectly. You will fulfill it by the means which God will inspire in you and by the exercise of the theological virtues, as I explained to you.

Resolutions

I give you these counsels as secondary resolutions:

1. Faithfulness to your three hours of prayer if your duties allow you. You should live in constant prayer, but be sure that time dedicated officially to the *intimate* and *loving* service for Jesus is very pleasing to Him.
2. Be careful to base your interior life on the intimate and special relations with the Holy Trinity which proceed from the mystical incarnation and its consequences. Follow the inspirations of the Holy Spirit in your interior life, but dwell always in God's bosom.
3. In relations with your neighbor, always see Jesus in him or her, and be always Jesus for him or her, as already explained.
4. Always take the things of God seriously.

Conclusion

Assuming that Our Lord Himself deigned to show you the purpose and fruit of this retreat, as we draw to its end we should contemplate and penetrate, with respect and love, the grace which the Lord has granted to you today. As happens with the things of God, when we offer a gift to the Lord, even though our *offering* seems to stand out, in reality, we receive more than we give. Our gift is more His *grace* than our doing. When we think that we are very generous to God, what happens is that we have been won over by His generosity. This is the delight and glory of our relationship with God, we are always won over; we feel the blessedness of our defeat; we always conclude by praising His victory, thanking Him for His munificence and annihilating ourselves before His love.

For this reason, our last word is thanksgiving in our relations with God; for this reason, the subject of Mass and of almost all liturgical acts is *thanksgiving*. In order to give thanks for the grace you have received today you must contemplate it in depth, even though we never manage to understand fully one single grace of God, since each one is like a link which connects to the great chain of the past, and links to an unending chain of the future and eternity. Besides, God, who is incomprehensible and unfathomable, gives Himself to the soul in each of His gifts.

The first result of today's grace is the divine delight. Jesus is pleased and so is the Trinity. Can you imagine a greater grace? Can the soul experience a purer and more complete joy?

After the infinite delight in Himself, there is no good that could be compared to the Lord's delight in His poor creatures, through Jesus and in Jesus. The satisfaction of love, the reward of our efforts, the supreme happiness of the soul is *to make God happy*. Relish your happiness in silence.

The glory of God, the consolation of Jesus and the repose of the Holy Spirit are in that delight. Enjoy that divine delight and be happy in the Lord's delight. Jesus is pleased. Do you need anything else to be happy?

The second grace linked with your offering of today is a more intimate union with Jesus. He is your love, your happiness, your all. Your only longing is to be united more closely with Him and now you are more united with Him. He is more yours and you are more His. You have penetrated more deeply into His Heart, that is, into His designs, desires, sentiments, sufferings and joys. It seems to me that now the beatings of your heart are the beatings of Jesus' Heart: beatings of purity, love, suffering, generosity, tenderness, delicacy and fruitfulness.

Embrace your Treasure; immerse yourself into its abyss and let yourself be embraced with its love; live by its Life; let yourself be permeated with its myrrh; empty yourself before your All; unite yourself closely, ineffably with your *only Love.*

The third grace is the blessing of fruitfulness; now you are more fruitful, because you are more Jesus Crucified; because He increased the purity, love and suffering of your soul, without your understanding it; because He dilated your heart so that priests and the Church could fit into it. In other words, you are Jesus to a greater extent and fullness.

Your spiritual children grew in number, but even though they are countless, Jesus is really the only one. Each son that Jesus gives you is like a new mystical incarnation of Jesus, or to say it more clearly, it is the one mystical incarnation which extends to all souls and into which your soul is immersed. One could say something like this: each son God gives you makes you *more mother* of Jesus. Isn't it true that you long for your spiritual children to be as numerous as the stars of the sky? Because those sons are priests, each one is a patriarch, father of a tribe and consequently, you are a mother of a tribe of souls. What fruitfulness is God giving you today, making you a mother of priests?

The fourth grace – isn't it the supreme one? – is the blessing of suffering, of the Cross you receive today more abundantly than ever, even though Our Lord has always lavishly poured His blessing into your soul.

A new cross, or rather always the same cross, the only Cross of Jesus, was given to you today with more perfection, not as a burden, but as a recompense.

The participation in Christ's Cross is the greatest recompense a soul can aspire to on earth. The beatific vision is the  recompense in eternity and the Cross, that recompense in time. The more frequently and the better a soul receives the Cross, the greater is its recompense and the more complete its bliss.

The Cross you receive now is the intimate Cross of the Heart of Jesus, with its most exquisite sweetness and bitterness. This is a priestly Cross; it is the quintessence of Jesus' priesthood. Priestly in its source, this Cross is produced by the most exquisite love for the Father and souls. Priestly in itself, it is formed by the purest substance of priestly love, which, in contact with the sins of the world, is transformed into immense priestly suffering. And it is priestly in its purpose, since its fruit is the extension, purification, sanctification and transformation of Christ's priests, who share in His unique and eternal Priesthood.

Many other graces are contained in and derived from today's outstanding grace, but it is enough to point out these four:

(1) God's delight.

(2) Closer union of your soul with Him.

(3) Greater and more perfect fruitfulness.

(4) More intimate participation in the intimate Cross of Jesus' Heart.

Isn't it true that what you have done today is very little, almost nothing, compared with what you have received? Isn't it true that Jesus' love gloriously won your love and His divine generosity won your generosity?

If He shows you His gratitude for what you have given Him, shouldn't you show Him yours much more? What thanksgiving should correspond to this chain of incomprehensible benefits?

Now you possess Jesus more than ever. So take Him and offer Him through Mary in thanksgiving. No matter how great the gifts you have received from God are, greater or so very great is the Gift you offer: Jesus. Given that this Gift is *yours*, offer it to the Father, and your thanksgiving will be perfect.

But offer it self-emptied; offer it with burning love; offer yourself in union with Him. Can the One be offered without the other?

Since Our Lord wanted to associate me in your marvelous work, I will also associate myself with your thanksgiving; and humiliated, loving, grateful and *self-offered*, let us offer Jesus – the real Eucharist – and let us recite the triumphal canticle of gratitude: *Te Deum laudamus....*

Personal Reflection of Conchita

THE END OF THE RETREAT

Concrete points of the Retreat

1. Sacrifice as a center of God's will.
2. I emptied myself and I don't belong to myself anymore; I must do the will of the Father with divine passion.
3. To adore, accept and love always and only God's will in all things.
4. To be at peace always, happy on tabors or on Calvaries, without alternatives or restrictions, submitting to whatever God may determine.
5. My life should be a faithful echo of the Father's will.
6. All, because He wants it, only to please Him. Loving joy in doing His will, even to sacrifice for Him and souls.
7. To joyfully accept God's will which tortures and immolates.
8. I will accept that divine will in spiritual children and in the Works.
9. I will accept being a victim *exposed* and *disposed* to whatever God wants, and being a mystical priest, offering Jesus, my spiritual children and myself.
10. The Cross is the supreme fulfillment of God's will; for this reason, it is the supreme martyrdom and joy.
    God put on the Cross the secret of suffering and joy.
11. I need *triumphal love* in my sorrows. May His will be done and not mine.
12. *Everything…* and the way the Father wants it.
13. I won't be master of my actions, nor of my life.
14. Faithfulness in abandonment.
15. The will of God will be the supreme motive of my actions, in their mode and details.
16. That torturing will be my martyrdom and joy.

17. To be Jesus! who looks through my eyes and I through His …who loves through me and I through Him…. May God's will in all its aspects be my happiness, my center and my entire bliss.
18. Neither look at myself, nor admire myself.
Exposed and *disposed* to the entire will of God.

December 8

I returned from Morelia and managed to assist at Mass and receive communion. The day was full of people, since it was my sixty-sixth birthday.

Lord, grant me at my death to have fulfilled Your designs for me.

CHART OF RETREATS OF CONCEPCIÓN CABRERA DE ARMIDA WITH BISHOP LUIS M. MARTÍNEZ 1925-1936

DATE	PLACE	WRITINGS	THEME AND GRACES OF THE EXERCISES
July 1-10, 1925	General House of the Sisters of the Cross of the Sacred Heart of Jesus	AC 45, 183-475 SE[129] 3, 215-216; 227-241	"Your Life in God" (cf. AC 45, 187; SE 3, 228). CCA makes a summary of the graces received from the Lord during her life (cf. AC 45, 217f). She starts her spiritual direction with Bishop Luis M. Martínez (cf. AC 45, 375).
July 16-25, 1926	Morelia, Mexico, Archbishop's residence	AC 47, 1-148	"Loving with the Holy Spirit" (cf. AC 47, 6). CCA is unified in love, loving with the Holy Spirit (cf. AC 47, 32).
September 9-17, 1927	Morelia, Mexico, Archbishop's residence	AC 48, 241-397	"To Be Mother" (cf. AC 48, 259). The Lord makes CCA an echo of His love and suffering (cf. AC 48, 248-250).
November 22-30, 1928	Morelia, Mexico, Archbishop's residence	AC 52, 296-400 AC 53, 1-63; 87-89	"To Be Jesus Crucified" (cf. AC 52, 297). CCA becomes aware of belonging to the Church and being a spiritual mother of priests (cf. AC 53, 13-41).
November 14-30, 1929	Morelia, Mexico, Archbishop's residence	AC 53, 338-401 AC 54, 1-347	"The Interior of the Heart of Jesus" (cf. AC 53, 346). The Lord conferred priestly graces on CCA to be communicated to others (cf. AC 54, 160; 245).
December 11-25, 1930	Morelia, Mexico, Archbishop's residence	AC 56, 15-281	"The Consummation in the Unity of the Holy Trinity" (cf. AC 56, 234). The Lord makes CCA a fire to burn vices and enkindle charity (cf. AC 56, 256).
December 25, 1931-January 14, 1932	Morelia, Mexico Archbishop's residence	AC 57, 283-400 AC 58, 1-400	"The Third Love" (cf. AC 58, 169). CCA lives the third love (cf. AC 57, 301). Together with the Blessed Virgin, she is present at Mass (cf. AC 58, 95).
March 6-25, 1933	Morelia, Mexico, Archbishop's residence	AC 59, 205-400 AC 60, 71-373 SE 4, 1-228	"The Reposes of Jesus" (cf. AC 59, 207). CCA receives light on the divinity of Jesus (cf. AC 59, 212). She should be light (cf. AC 59, 219).

July 28-August 21, 1934	Morelia, Mexico, Archbishop's residence	AC 61, 226-399 AC 62, 1-65; 70-358 SE 4, 230-451	"To Offer Jesus to Be Crucified" (cf. AC 62, 97). CCA should crucify Jesus and crucify herself in union with Him in order to give Him to priests (cf. AC 62, 253-324).
October 14-November 18, 1935	Morelia, Mexico, Archbishop's residence	AC 63, 203-371 AC 64, 1-192 AC 65, 5-28	"The Mystical Incarnation" (cf. AC 64, 14). All for the glory of the Father (cf. AC 64, 39-40). Crusade on behalf of Families (cf. AC 63, 344).
October 3-November 2, 1936	Morelia, Mexico, Archbishop's residence	AC 65, 162-398 AC 66, 1-175 SE 4, 495-516	"The Perfect Joy" (cf. AC 65, 214). CCA participated in the interior Cross of Jesus (cf. AC 65, 216). She sensed that it was the last time in her life she would make her retreat (cf. AC 65, 327; 66, 29).

ENDNOTES

1 The Works of the Cross consists of five associations: (1) the Apostolate of the Cross, founded on May 3, 1895; (2) the Sisters of the Cross of the Sacred Heart of Jesus, founded on May 3, 1897, as an institute of contemplative women of perpetual adoration who offer their lives especially for the sanctification of priests; (3) the Covenant of Love with the Sacred Heart of Jesus, founded on November 30, 1909, which gathers together lay people who commit themselves to seek perfection within their lay vocations according to the Spirituality of the Cross; (4) the Fraternity of Christ the Priest, which was founded on January 19, 1912, for bishops and priests; (5) the Missionaries of the Holy Spirit, founded by Fr. Felix Rougier on December 25, 1914, as a clerical religious congregation dedicated to priestly ministries and to the spiritual direction of souls.

2 Conchita wrote her *Account of Conscience* (entitled in Spanish, *Cuenta de Conciencia*) by order of her spiritual directors in the course of 43 years (1893-1936). The abbreviation *AC* is used herein to refer to this diary. The writings we present in this volume of the Retreat are excerpts from her *Account of Conscience*, Volumes 52, 295-401 and 53, 2-89.

3 *Vida* I [Life], 46, Private edition.

4 *Autobiografía* I [Autobiography] I, 13b, Private edition.

5 The Servant of God Archbishop Luis M. Martínez Rodríguez (1881-1956) held various responsible positions in the Church. He was Rector of the Seminary in Morelia, Apostolic Administrator of Chilapa, Auxiliary Bishop in Morelia, Archbishop of Mexico City and Primate of Mexico and member of the Mexican Academy of Languages. His spiritual writings manifest sound doctrine, great personal holiness, serenity and optimism to such an extent that he was called the "Archbishop Peacemaker." He was spiritual director not only to the Venerable Conchita Armida, but also to many other outstanding personalities of his time. Because of his reputation for holiness of life, the process for his beatification was opened in 1985.

6 The Archbishop of Morelia, Leopoldo Ruiz y Flores, insisted in his letter to Conchita of September 30, 1923, that she should seek spiritual direction from his Auxiliary Bishop, L.M. Martínez, because he felt that Bishop Martínez would be the right spiritual director for her.

7 *Notas íntimas* [Intimate Notes], Ed. La Cruz, México, 1971, p. 313.

8 Concepción Cabrera de Armida, *Ser Jesus Crucificado*, Ejercicios Espirituales 1928, Ediciones Cimiento, Mexico, 1996, November 26, p. 62.

9 *Canticle*, stanza 27, 3: *The Collected Works of St. John of the Cross*, translated by Kieran Kavanaugh, OCD, and Otilio Rodriguez, OCD, revised edition (1991).

10 *AC* 2, 62: 1894.

11 *AC* 4, 288: 1894.

12 *AC* 4, 369: 1894.

13 *AC* 3, 49; 4, 5: 1894.

14 Cf. *AC* 6, 97: 1895 and 66, 18: 1936.

15 *Canticle*, stanza 37, 3.

16 *AC* 65, 354; 65, 346: 1936.

17 Concepción Cabrera de Armida contemplated the Cross of the Apostolate in a vision (January of 1894). It is the symbol that sums up the Spirituality of the Cross, which animates and gives life to the Works of the Cross. Conchita described this vision: "I was in deep prayer when suddenly I saw an immense image of living light. Its center was brilliant. How strange – a white light! Above this immensity of light with thousands of rays of what seemed to be gold and fire, I saw a dove with its wings extended, somehow covering that torrent of light. I saw everything very clearly, since it was light. Two or three days later, again I saw a white dove in the midst of the great fire which had clear and very brilliant rays of light. In the center was the dove, again with wings extended, and below it at the far end of the immense light, a very large Cross with a Heart at the center-point, between the extended arms" (*Vida* [Life] I, 211-214; cf. *AC* 1, 434; *Apostolado de la Cruz* [Apostolate of the Cross], 377-378).

18 *AC* 4, 93: 1894; 6, 120: 1895. The mystery of the unity in the Trinity was broadly developed in 1913, when she received special lights on that subject from the Lord. The retreat of 1930 was centered on that mystery.

19 *AC* 6, 123: 1895.

20 *AC* 6, 102: 1895; 1, 463: 1894.

21 *AC* 1, 514 and 554: 1894. *Confidences*, written in 1927-1930, contain the beautiful message of the Lord to priests, in which He urges them to holiness and transformation into Christ. Jesus explains the dignity of the priesthood and all the dangers priests undergo. Cf. Concepción Cabrera de Armida, *Sacerdotes de Cristo* (Priests of Christ), Editorial La Cruz, Mexico, 2004.

22 *AC* 5, 108-109: 1895.

23 *AC* 12, 36: 1900.

24 *AC* 25, 138-139: 1907.

25 Cf. *AC* 19, 307-308: 1903.

26 *AC* 6, 73 and 102: 1895.

27 *AC* 6, 103: 1895; 23, 154: 1906.

28 *AC* 6, 105-106 and 108: 1895; *AC* 38, 65: 1914.

29 *AC* 6, 109: 1895.

30 *AC* 1, 184: 1894.

31 *AC* 1, 105 and 188: 1894.

32 *AC* 1, 143 and 186: 1894.

33 *AC* 1, 191 and 278: 1894.

34 See note 17.

35 *AC* 6, 251: 1895; *Apostolado de la Cruz,* 43.

36 *AC* 1, 395 and 389: 1894.

37 *AC* 36, 106: 1912.

38 *AC* 1, 348; 1, 444c-d: 1894.

39 C. Cabrera de Armida, *Tesoro* [Treasure], Private Edition, p. 97. *AC* 1, 236: 1894.

40 *Autobiography,* 2, 91.

41 *AC* 2, 1: 1894.

42 C. Cabrera de Armida, *Apostolado de la Cruz*, 6a-7.

43 C. Cabrera de Armida, *Tesoro,* 12-13. The diminutive of the name Concepción is Concha, which also means "shell," or "mother-of-pearl." Jesus used to say that He was a pearl hidden in His Concha ("shell").

44 *Autobiography* 1, 51.

45 *AC* 17, 361-362: January 14, 1902.

46 *Autobiography* 2, 32-35.

47 *Vida* [Life] 1, 208-210.

48 *Ibid.*, 40.

49 The Lord referred to the cloistered Sisters of the Cross of the Sacred Heart of Jesus which Conchita had founded as the Oasis, a place of life and rest in the desert.

50 *AC* 4, 198-199: 1894.

51 *AC* 4, 277: 1894.

52 *AC* 23, 18-19: 1906.

53 *AC* 22, 192: 1906. Cf. Juan Gutiérrez, M.Sp.S., *Concepción Cabrera de Armida, Cruz de Jesús, Vida mística e itinerario espiritual,* T. I, Editorial La Cruz, México, 1998. Laura Linares R., RCSCJ, *La Encarnación Mística y su dinamismo en Concepción Cabrera de Armida*, Ediciones Cimiento, México, 2006.

54 *AC* 45, 435-439: June 8, 1925; 63, 257 and 266: October 1935; 66, 64-66: October 25, 1936.

55 Cf. *AC* 40, 292-294, 298-302: June 6, 1916.

56 "Your role is that of living the Mass mystically, and that should also be that of the Oasis, to continue the offertory, offering Me to the Father and offering yourself in union with Me, and thus arriving at the consecration, repeating in union with Me and My infinite merits: 'This is My Body; this is My Blood'" (*AC* 46, 85-88: October 20, 1925).

57 Cf. *AC* 41, 274: June 16, 1917; *AC* 42, 281-283: June 22, 1918.

58 Cf. *AC* 41, 217-219: June 11, 1917.

59 *AC* 45, 206-208: July 3, 1925.

60 Cf. *AC* 64, 38a-39a: October 20, 1935.

61 *AC* 66, 30-32: 1936.

62 The city of Morelia, Mexico, is consecrated to the Sacred Heart of Jesus.

63 Miss Dolores Buitrón, familiarly called Lolita, was the sister of Canon Juan B. Buitrón who was an intimate friend of Bishop L.M. Martínez.

64 Bishop Luis M. Martínez Rodríguez, then Auxiliary Bishop of Morelia.

65 Bishop Martínez makes Conchita aware of the graces she received in her life and God's plan for her. The goal set before her in the retreat of 1928 is "*to be Jesus Crucified with His intimate sentiments.*" It is the result of Jesus' designs for Conchita in making her an "*echo of His love and sorrows*" (*AC* 48, 248). Thus, the wonderful unity of God's action in her may be noted.

66 In her retreat with Fr. José G. Treviño, M.Sp.S., from 13 to 19 of September 1921, Conchita wrote: "*What is the color, the ray of Jesus-Light which should predominate in me? It is this: 'To know nothing except Jesus, and Him crucified.' To be another Jesus crucified. This is the fruit which God asks of me, the*

flower He wants to sniff. I must reproduce Jesus in me by means of the transforming virtues, that is, through the Cross, which assimilates me more to Him. He wants me to be Jesus, but not the Christ in the poverty of Bethlehem, nor the Christ in His hidden life of Nazareth, nor the zealous Christ in His public life, but the Christ in ignominy, abandonment and crucifixion on Calvary and in the Eucharist" (*AC* 43, 138: September 16, 1921).

67 Every volume of the Venerable Conchita's retreats with Archbishop Martínez has a particular style according to her interior needs at the time. Basically, it is composed of the Archbishop's meditations and Conchita's reflections. In some places she casually inter-mingled parts of the Bishop's meditations with her own responses, making her words and insights sometimes a bit difficult to present in a systematic way. In this volume, the distribution of meditations and reflections corresponds to the original text.

68 There are many texts in Conchita's *Account of Conscience* which underline that it is Jesus dwelling in her soul who attracts the gaze of the Father: "*If I love you with predilection*" – the Lord would tell her years later, during her spiritual retreat in 1933 – "*it is because I see something of My Father in you, and this something strongly attracts Me. Just as the Father sees and loves all things in Me, I too have all My joy in My Father, and I see all things in this beloved Father*" (*AC* 59, 218-220). In 1894, Conchita received the fontal grace of her life, from which all other graces would proceed. She wrote: "*One day, [while I was] in the Church of Our Lady of Mount Carmel, the Lord told me: 'The Father is gazing upon you,' and I felt bathed, electrified and annihilated*" (*Vida* [Life] 1, 286-287). Years later, retrospectively reviewing her life, she wrote: "*You said to me 'the Father is gazing upon you,' and from that moment His reflection remained in my soul, and You and the divine will also remained in it*" (*AC* 59, 224-227).

69 Bishop Luis M. Martínez Rodríguez.

70 From her first retreat in 1889, Conchita became aware that "her mission is to save souls." Near the end of her life, on February 15, 1935, Jesus told her: "*Let me use your heart as it pleases Me, because you do not belong to yourself. You belong to My Church; you are all Mine and I know how to use you in union with Me for the glory of the Father and on behalf of souls*" (cf. *AC* 63, 59-60).

71 Cf. Concepción Cabrera de Armida, *Loving with the Holy Spirit*, Editrice Libreria Vaticana, 2007.

72 Referring to Bishops Leopoldo L. Flores and Luis M. Martínez.

73 On February 5, 1911, the year characterized by Conchita's particular love for the Church, the Lord explained to her: "*You no longer belong to yourself, you belong to the Church, and the Word will make use of you for her sake. Alone you are worth nothing, but in union with Me, God will do great things through you*" (*AC* 35, 36-38; cf. R. de la Rosa, M.Sp.S., *En favor de tu Iglesia amada*, Ed. Concar, Mexico, 1972).

74 *AC* 48, 337-344: "*The mission of giving Jesus.*"

75 Conchita wrote in her *Account of Conscience* (12, 225-228: April 3, 1900): "*I have the certitude that the Lord gave me the gift of purity during my entire life. I have understood it only now with a moral certainty which does not allow me to doubt. I never had a single impure movement in thought. However, I understand this virtue only in general.*" She always had a special love for this virtue

(*AC* 56, 332-334). In spite of this, she feels herself to be a sinner when she sees herself in the light of God, because under this light, she experiences God's holiness (cf. J.M. Padilla, *Concepción Cabrera de Armida*, II, Ed. La Cruz, 1982, pp. 134-135).

76 Cf. the retreat of 1927 on the subject of *To Be a Mother*. The Lord made Conchita understand that mystical motherhood "*is the very fruitfulness of the Father which is bestowed on the soul by the Holy Spirit*" (*AC* 47, 279-282).

77 After nine years of preparation, on March 25, 1906, the grace of the mystical incarnation was granted to Conchita. See "Introduction" p. xxixff.

78 Since Conchita had so many experiences of desolation of the spirit, the Lord could give to His Church a real treatise on desolation which shows her to be a mistress of the spiritual life who teaches from her own life experience (*AC* 16, 137-223: 1900).

79 Fr. Felix Rougier (1859-1938) was the founder of the Missionaries of the Holy Spirit (December 25, 1914).

80 In *The Living Flame of Love*, St. John of the Cross wrote about spiritual directors: "Not everyone capable of hewing the wood knows how to carve the statue, nor does everyone able to carve know how to perfect and polish the work, nor do all who know how to polish it know how to paint it, nor do all who can paint it know how to put the finishing touches on it and bring the work to completion. One can do with the statue only what one knows how to do, and when craftsmen try to do more than they know how to do, the statue is ruined" (stanza 3, 57). In her spiritual journey Conchita was guided by many outstanding priests and bishops: Father Alberto Cuscó y Mir, S.J. (1893-1903), Father Felix Rougier, Archbishop Ramón Ibarra y González (1912-1917), Bishop Emeterio Valverde (1917-1925) and Archbishop Luis M. Martínez (1925-1937). Each one of her spiritual directors had a very important role in her life.

81 The Trinitarian character of Conchita's whole life and of her teaching is one of the most profound aspects of her spirituality (*AC* 8, 268-269; 9, 329-330).

82 Heb 10:5.

83 Lk 22:42.

84 Jn 8:29.

85 Lk 22:42.

86 Conchita was in the habit of imposing bodily mortifications on herself as an aid to her spiritual growth. One of these frequently repeated mortifications involved prostrating herself on a bed of thorny branches, which she called "roses." See, for example, *AC* 3, 46.

87 He refers to Archbishop Leopoldo Ruiz Flores who was exiled in Texas, USA, because of the religious persecution.

88 Conchita received the Lord's *Confidences* on the priesthood beginning with her retreat of 1927 (Morelia), directed by Archbishop Martínez (cf. *To Be a Mother*, Ed. Cimiento, Mexico, 1996, p. 79; cf. J. Esquerda Bifet, *The Priesthood of Christ and the Ministerial Priesthood in the Experience and Message of Concepción Cabrera de Armida*, Ed. Cimiento, Mexico, 1995).

89 Heb 9:14.

90 "*To be a Mother*! These words contain God's designs for you." Cf. Retreat of 1927, *To Be a Mother*, Ed. Cimiento, Mexico, 1996; *AC* 48, 252.

91 Gal 4:19.

92 1 Cor 3:2.

93 2 Cor 11:29.

94 2 Cor 13:4-7.

95 Literally *cathedra*, which is a university chair or teaching position.

96 *Labarum* (Latin), an imperial standard of the later Roman emperors resembling the *vexillum*; especially, the standard adopted by Constantine after his conversion to Christianity, consisting of a purple silk banner hanging from a crosspiece on a pike and surmounted by a golden crown bearing the Chi-Rho [the cross and the monogram of the first two letters of the word Christ in Greek].

97 Concepción Cabrera de Armida contemplated the Cross of the Apostolate in a vision in January of 1894. It is the symbol that sums up the Spirituality of the Cross. It explicitly conveys the redemptive love of Christ, Priest and Victim, which in itself is a revelation of the love of the Father, who gives His Son to be led by the Holy Spirit to the Cross in order to accomplish the redemption of humanity. Jesus joined many graces to that Cross and explained to Conchita that it was the edifice of perfection: that all mysteries, gifts and fruits of the Holy Spirit were there. It has the power to snatch thousands of souls from the claws of the devil and has the power to cure souls and bodies (*AC* 6, 251-252).

98 During the crucial battle with Maxentius near Rome (313), on the Milvian bridge, Constantine received the apparition of the Cross with this inscription: "*In hoc signo vinces*" (In this sign you shall conquer). Afterwards, he promulgated the famous Edict of Milan, by which he granted freedom to the Church.

99 Jesus guided Conchita gradually to realize His work in her. In the course of her retreat of 1921 with Fr. José G. Treviño, M.Sp.S., she meditated on that mystery in her life: "I should reproduce Jesus Crucified in me. And what is the profound meaning of Jesus Crucified? In respect to His Father, the substance of His crucifixion is *abandonment* – of Jesus to the Father... placing Himself unconditionally in His hands; of the Father to Jesus, leaving Him in the most cruel desolation.... One must ponder over the ineffable bliss of the Divine Word while He is gazed upon by His Father who was His delight, His life, His all, His other Self; (our beatitude shares in His gaze). Then what would be the infinite suffering of Jesus in His abandonment by the one whom He loved most? His unspeakable suffering achieved the summit! Hell itself is rejection, the abandonment by God that Jesus wanted to experience to purchase *fortitude* for us! What did Jesus say amidst this infinite sea of bitterness, refusal and hatred (because of the sins He was bearing in atonement)? 'Father, into Your hands I commend My spirit!' Heroic confidence, in sublime degree, the summit of love! A psalm says: 'Even if He puts me to death, I will trust in Him.' The ray of light, the culminating color which God wants from me is this: *I abandon myself to God who abandons me!* That is the degree of perfection that God wants from me. Supreme abandonment, generosity and the confidence of Christ! This is to lean on the very Cross! Total abandonment, the last stroke of love! Oh Divine Abandoned One, I will call on You in my abandonment!" (*AC* 43, 138-139: September 16, 1921).

100 This is a reference to Bishop Luis M. Martínez Rodríguez.

101 Mr. Augustine Lagüera was married to Maria Ulíbarri. They were very pious

persons and good friends of Bishop Martínez. They had two houses which could communicate interiorly; they lived in one of them, and the other one, furnished, was empty. During the persecution, Bishop Martínez was hidden in it. In Morelia, no one knew where the Bishop was. Conchita used to go to this place to do her annual retreat. The Sisters of the Cross joked that the Bishop went to *Anemurio*, the place of which he was titular bishop.

102 Conchita wrote these words of Jesus in her *Account of Conscience* (27, 58): "*One of the purposes of My direction with you is to show experts on the spiritual life to what extent My goodness abounds in a soul who allows Me to fashion it.*"

103 Referring to Bishop L.M. Martínez Rodríguez.

104 Leopoldo Ruiz y Flores, Archbishop of Morelia (1911-1941), was the Apostolic Delegate (1929-1937) during the religious persecution. He was a great protector of the Works of the Cross and spiritual director of Concepción Cabrera de Armida and Fr. Felix Rougier, Missionary of the Holy Spirit.

105 Due to the religious persecution, many bishops were exiled.

106 *Confidences*, written in 1927-1930, contain the beautiful message of the Lord to priests, in which He urges them on to holiness and transformation in Christ. Jesus explains the dignity of the priesthood and all the dangers priests undergo. See note 88 (November 25th).

107 St. Catherine of Siena.

108 This is a reference to Bishop Martínez.

109 Cf. *AC* 6, 64; 12, 98-99. Bishop Martínez told her: "*To be blind and to be enlightened are not contrary. In fact, in order to be abandoned to God's will, the soul must have much light to know into whose hands it places itself, into what Heart it casts itself, and to what will it abandons itself*" (*AC* 46, 40: 1925).

110 In the course of her process of purification, which Conchita had to endure in order to attain to the union with Christ through the exercises of Jesus' virtues reflected in her own life, Jesus asked of her constantly "*not to lose peace*" (cf. *AC* 3, 53: April 26, 1894); that "*there is no other way to find peace, but to make war on oneself*" (cf. *AC* 13, 151-154); that "*He needs her in peace in order to communicate Himself to her*" (cf. *AC* 60, 397-398; 61, 12).

111 Through Him, with Him, in Him, in the unity of the Holy Spirit, all glory and honor is Yours, almighty Father, for ever and ever.

112 Here finishes this part of the *Account of Conscience* 52, 295-401 (November 1928). The following texts belong to volume 53.

113 Here there is a bit of confusion with regard to the dates given in the original writings. In any case, it does not change the content of her thought.

114 The mystical incarnation bears within itself the fruitfulness of the Father (cf. *AC* 38, 93-98; 55, 140-153).

115 The grace of the mystical incarnation was the theme of the retreat directed by Fr. José G. Treviño (26 December 1923 - 2 January 1924), and it was very important in Conchita's life, because she received the necessary light to live that grace. She became aware of the "unifying principle of her life": "*I need only one thing! To enter fully into this great grace of the mystical incarnation, which the infinite love of God has bestowed on me. The goal of these graces is to make me priest, victim and altar*" (cf. *AC* 44, 137b-138b). In 1935, Archbishop Martínez explained to her: "*The source of your life is God, in whose*

loving bosom you will enter in eternity, but from now, you should enter as much as possible on this earth. Yet the primary source of your life is the outstanding grace of the mystical incarnation, which you received thirty years ago and which sprang forth, so to speak, from the inmost depth of your soul, as a fountain welling up to eternal life. Everything you have received from God after that grace, all the numerous and fruitful stages which your spirit has passed through during these thirty years, are but the development of that precious grace" (*AC* 63, 244-256: October 17, 1935).

116 As the fruit of the retreat given by Fr. Treviño, Conchita wrote: "*The best thing I can do for the Works of the Cross is to live the mystical incarnation*" (cf. *AC* 44, 138b-140b).

117 See notes 88 and 106.

118 Cf. *AC* 35, 36-40; 37, 18-19.

119 In virtue of the presence of the Incarnate Word in Conchita, a sort of "*amplification*" takes place and it corresponds to a generation of priestly souls in her (cf. *AC* 53, 9-19; 54, 395-397; 55, 11; 56, 281, 291-293, 369-374; 61, 46-54; 64, 12a-14; cf. Retreat of 1927, *Ser Madre* [To Be a Mother], Ed. Cimiento, México, 1996, p. 12).

120 Ph 4:13: "I can do all things through Him who strengthens me."

121 2 Cor 12:10: "for when I am weak, then I am strong."

122 The Lord made Conchita understand: "*I will never abandon you, even though you don't see Me, even though you don't feel Me... I want you to accompany Me in the prayer of the Garden. Let Me work in you. Don't you see what I want by this? To lead you to do the Father's will in everything. I never showed this better than in My prayer in the Garden*" (*AC* 1, 130; 133-135). Later on, the Lord told her: "*I needed to take you to the Garden because, otherwise, how could we meet together if you did not know the place?*" (*AC* 1, 414: 1894).

123 Jn 17:21-23.

124 On February 20, 1935, the Lord reminded Conchita: "Don't think that the mystical incarnation in your soul has already passed; rather, it *is always present*; it is continuously being accomplished by the fruitfulness of the Father and the cooperation of the Holy Spirit" (*AC* 63, 69).

125 This must be understood in an analogical sense. In the strict sense, Jesus is the first priest and, while Mary shares uniquely in His priesthood, she is not a priest in the ministerial sense.

126 Francisco, Manuel, Ignacio, Salvador and Guadalupe Armida Cabrera.

127 Cf. *AC* 48, 248, retreat of 1927, *Ser Madre* [To Be a Mother].

128 Jesus refers to Bishop Luis M. Martínez.

129 *Directed Retreats* of Concepción Cabrera de Armida, unpublished work of four volumes, which contain the fifty-four retreats made by Conchita during her life.

WORKS BY ARCHBISHOP LUIS M. MARTÍNEZ AND CONCEPCIÓN CABRERA DE ARMIDA

Luis M. Martínez, *Secrets of the Interior Life*, Sophia Institute Press, Manchester, 2003.

Luis M. Martínez, *True Devotion of the Holy Spirit* (former title: *The Sanctifier*), Sophia Institute Press, Manchester, 2000.

Luis M. Martínez, *When Jesus Sleeps*, Sophia Institute Press, Manchester, 2000.

Luis M. Martínez, *Only Jesus*, John Paul II Institute of Christian Spirituality, 2001.

Luis M. Martínez, *Spread Your Wings*, Ediciones Cimiento, Printed in Acme Printing, Modesto, CA, 2002.

Luis M. Martínez, *Meditations for Christmas*, A Spiritual Retreat as a Preparation for Christmas, Ediciones Cimiento, Printed in Acme Printing, Modesto, CA, 2001.

Concepción Cabrera de Armida, *Before the Altar: A Hundred Visits to Jesus in the Blessed Sacrament*, CMJ Marian Publishers, 2001.

Concepción Cabrera de Armida, *I Am: Eucharistic Meditations on the Gospel*, ST PAULS / Alba House, 2001.

Concepción Cabrera de Armida, *Irresistibly Drawn to the Eucharist*, ST PAULS / Alba House, 2002.

Fr. M.M. Philipon, O.P., *Conchita: A Mother's Spiritual Diary*, ST PAULS / Alba House, 1978.

Concepción Cabrera de Armida, *You Belong to the Church*, Pilgrimage to Rome 1913, Libreria Editrice Vaticana, 1999.

Concepción Cabrera de Armida, *Under the Gaze of the Father*, Retreat Directed by Archbishop Luis M. Martínez on the Grace of the Mystical Incarnation, 1935, ST PAULS / Alba House, 2011.

Concepción Cabrera de Armida, *Loving with the Holy Spirit*, Retreat Directed by Bishop Luis M. Martínez, 1926, Libreria Editrice Vaticana, 2007.

Concepción Cabrera de Armida, *A Mother's Letters: A Vision of Faith in Everyday Life*, ST PAULS / Alba House, 2004.

Concepción Cabrera de Armida, *Seasons of the Soul*, ST PAULS / Alba House, 2005.

Concepción Cabrera de Armida, *Holy Hours*, ST PAULS / Alba House, 2006.

Concepción Cabrera de Armida, *Roses and Thorns*, ST PAULS / Alba House, 2007.

Concepción Cabrera de Armida, *To My Priests*, Archangel Crusade of Love, Cleveland, 1996.

For Further Information

Religiose della Croce del Sacro Cuore di Gesù
Via Appia Nuova, 1468
00178 Roma, Italia
Tel/Fax: 06-7-934-0094
e-mail: relcroce@pcn.net

Religiosas de la Cruz del Sagrado Corazón de Jesús
Francisco Sosa, 105
Col. Coyoacán
04000 Mexico, D.F., Mexico
Tel: 554-0011; Fax: 554-0335
e-mail: cimientocoyo@hotmail.com

Sisters of the Cross of the Sacred Heart of Jesus
1320 Maze Blvd.
Modesto, CA 95351 USA
Tel/Fax: 1-209-526-3525

Missionaries of the Holy Spirit
Christ the Priest Vicariate
U.S. Headquarters
P.O. Box 956
Garden Grove, CA 92842-0956 USA
Tel. (714) 534-5476
Fax. (714) 534-5184

This book was produced by ST PAULS/Alba House, the Society of St. Paul, an international religious congregation of priests and brothers dedicated to serving the Church through the communications media.

For information regarding this and associated ministries of the Pauline Family of Congregations, write to the Vocation Director, Society of St. Paul, 2187 Victory Blvd., Staten Island, New York 10314-6603. Phone (718) 982-5709; or E-mail: vocation@stpauls.us or check our internet site, www.vocationoffice.org